Magic, Divination, And Demonology Among The Hebrews And Their Neighbours: Including An Examination Of Biblical References And Of The Biblical Terms...

Thomas Witton Davies

MAGIC, DIVINATION,

AND

DEMONOLOGY

MAGIC, DIVINATION,

AND

DEMONOLOGY

AMONG THE HEBREWS AND THEIR NEIGHBOURS

INCLUDING AN

EXAMINATION OF BIBLICAL REFERENCES

AND OF THE

BIBLICAL ·TERMS

BY

T. WITTON DAVIES, B.A. (Lond.), Ph.D. (Leip.)

PROFESSOR OF OLD TESTAMENT LITERATURE, NORTH WALES BAPTIST COLLEGE
BANGOR; LECTURER IN SEMITIC LANGUAGES, UNIVERSITY COLLEGE, BANGOR;
MEMBER OF THE FOLLOWING SOCIETIES: ROYAL ASIATIC; BIBLICAL
ARCHÆOLOGY; GERMAN ORIENTAL; FRENCH ASIATIC; AND
FELLOW OF THE ANTHROPOLOGICAL INSTITUTE

LONDON

JAMES CLARKE & CO., 13 AND 14, FLEET STREET, E.C.

LEIPZIC

M. SPIRGATIS, MARIEN STRASSE, 23

LONDON
PRINTED BY GILBERT AND RIVINGTON, LTD.
ST. JOHN'S HOUSE, CLERKENWELL, E.C.

DEDICATED

TO MY WIFE

WITH AFFECTION AND GRATITUDE

PREFACE

THIS treatise was presented to the University of Leipzig, July, 1897, according to the rule requiring such a dissertation to be presented and accepted before the candidate is allowed to proceed to the examinations prescribed for the degree of Doctor of Philosophy in the University. The dissertation has to be printed and 200 copies presented to the University within one year from the time when the final examination was passed. The limits of time and of space, and the need that the dissertation should be printed essentially as it was accepted by the Philosophical faculty of the University, made it impossible to introduce much change. Since writing it, however, I have read and thought a great deal about the subjects with which my dissertation deals; some slight results of that will be seen in the correction of my MS. as well as in references to books newly published. Further results—results too, I hope, of continued reading and reflection—may show themselves at a future time.

The "Vita" or "Life" is left at the end, as it had to be printed in the copies sent to the University.

I will not close this preface without warmly acknowledging the uniform courtesy and kindness received from the Professors of the celebrated University of Leipzig whose classes I joined. I would like especially to acknowledge my indebtedness to Prof. Socin, one of the greatest living teachers of Arabic. Dr. Dillman, of Berlin, and Dr. Socin, of Leipzig, were teachers at least as great as any I have known, and I am thankful to an ever kind Providence to have been able to benefit from their instruction, and from their example of industry and thoroughness.

T. WITTON DAVIES.

MIDLAND BAPTIST COLLEGE, } NOTTINGHAM.
UNIVERSITY COLLEGE,
   Aug. 12, 1898.

CONTENTS

BOOKS AND EDITIONS CONSULTED OR REFERRED TO (WITH ABBREVIATIONS)

D'Alviella. (Hibbert) Lectures on the Origin and Growth of the Conception of God. London, 1892.

Anz. Zur Frage nach dem Ursprunge des Gnostizismus Wilhelm Anz. Leipzig, 1896.

Baudissen. Studien zur semitischen Religionsgeschichte von Wolf Wilhelm Grafen Baudissen. Leipzig, 1876 and 1878. 2 vols.

Bochartus, Sam. Hierozoicon. Editio Tertiæ. Lugd. et Traj. 1682.

Bousset. The Antichrist Legend. By W. Bousset. Translated by A. H. Keane. London, 1896.

Brecher. Das transcendentale Magie und magische Heilarten im Talmud. Wien, 1850.

Brewster. Letters on Natural Magic. By Sir David Brewster, K.H., &c. London, 5th edition, 1842.

Brinton. Religions of Primitive Peoples. By D. G. Brinton, LL.D., &c. London and New York, 1897.

Burton. Anatomy of Melancholy. By Henry Burton. London, 1861.

Caird. The Evolution of Religion. Gifford Lectures. By Edward Caird. 2 vols. Glasgow, 1893.

Caird J. An Introduction to the Philosophy of Religion. By John Caird. Glasgow, 1880.

Caldwell. Dravidian Grammar. By Bishop Caldwell. (Page 518 ff. Demonology among the Dravidians.)

Charles. The Book of Enoch. By R. H. Charles. Oxford, 1893.

Crook. Folk-lore of Northern India. By W. Crook. 2 vols. 2nd ed. London, 1896.

Delitzsch, Fried. Prolegomena, &c. Von Dr. Fried. Delitzsch. Leipzig, 1886.

Delitzsch, Franz (father). Various Commentaries and Articles in Dictionaries.

Dennys. The Folk-lore of China. By B. N. Dennys. London, 1876.

Doughty. Travels in Arabia Deserta. 2 vols. By C. M. Doughty. Cambridge, 1888.

Edersheim. Life and Times of the Messiah. By Alfred Edersheim. London, 1888.

Eisenmenger. Entdectes Judenthum. 2 vols. By J. A. Eisenmenger. Königsberg, 1711, 1714.

Ency. Brit. Encyclopædia Britannica. 9th edition.

Ennemoser. The History of Magic. By Joseph Ennemoser. Englished by Wm. Howitt. 2 vols. London, 1854.

Ewald. Die Lehre der Bibel von Gott. 4 vols. Leipzig, 1871–76.

Findlay. The Epistles to the Thessalonians, with Introduction, Notes, &c. By Rev. G. G. Findlay, M.A. Cambridge, 1896.

Frazer. The Golden Bough. A Study in Comparative Religion. By J. G. Frazer. 2 vols. London, 1890.

Freytag. Einleitung in das Studium der arabischen Sprache. Von G. W. Freytag. Bonn, 1861.

Gesenius. 1. Thesaurus.

2. Lexicon. 12th edition. Buhl.

3. Hebräische Grammatik. 26te Ausgabe. (Kautsch.) Leipzig, 1896. (An English Translation published by Clarendon Press at £1 1s. has just made its appearance. Why not at a price which students might be expected to afford? The German edition cost me bound, with discount, about 5s. 8d., and the English

edition includes no more, though it is better printed and also bound.)

Ginsburg. The Kabbalah. London, 1865.

Goldziher. Abhandlungen zur arabischen Philologie. Von Ignaz Goldziher : erste Theil. Leiden, 1896.

Granger. The Worship of the Romans. By F. Granger, D.Lit. London, 1895.

Grant. The Mysteries of all Nations. By Jas. Grant. Leith, 1880.

Grimm. Teutonic Mythology. By Jacob Grimm. 4 vols. (Continuous paging.) English translation. By J. S. Stallybrass. London, 1882—1888.

Hegel. Vorlesungen über die Philosophie der Religion. 2te Ausgabe. Berlin, 1840.

Herzog[1] } Real Encyclopädie. By Herzog, &c. 1st and 2nd
Herzog[2] }   editions respectively.

Hillebrandt. Ritualliteratur. Vedische Opfer und Zauber. Strassburg, 1897.

Horst. Zauberbibliothek : 6 Theile von G. C. Horst. Mainz. 1821—1826.

Hughes. Dictionary of Islam. By. T. P. Hughes. London, 1885.

Jahn. Der Aberglaube des bösen Blicks bei den Alten. Abhand. der sachs. Academ. der Wissenschaft. 1855.

Jevons. An introduction to the History of Religion. By Frank Byrom Jevons. London, 1896.

Joel. Der Aberglaube und die Stellung des Judensthums zu demselben. Von Rabbi David Joel. Parts 1 and 2. Breslau, 1881 and 1883.

Josephus, Works of. English Translation by Whiston.

King. Babylonian Magic and Sorcery, being the "prayers of the lifting up of the hands." By L. King. London, 1896.

Kohut. Jüdische Angel. u. Dämonologie. Von A. Kohut. Leipzig, 1866.

Lane. The Thousand and One Nights. By E. W. Lane. 3 vols. London, 1839.

Lang. 1. Myth, Ritual and Religion. By Andrew Lang. 2 vols. London, 1887.

2. Custom and Myth. By Andrew Lang. London, 1897.

3. The Making of Religion. By Andrew Lang. London, 1898.

Lenormant. 1. Chaldean Magic. By F. Lenormant. London, 1877.

2. Divination, et la science des presages. Par F. Lenormant. Paris, 1875.

Levy. Neu hebräisches u. chaldäisches Wörterbuch. Von Prof. Dr. Jacob Levy. 4 vols. Leipzig, 1876 to 1889.

Lyall. Asiatic Studies, Religious and Social. By Sir Alfred C. Lyall, K.C.B., C.I.E. London, 1882.

Meiners. Geschichte aller Religionen. By Prof. Meiners. 2 vols. 1806.

Michaelis, J. D. Commentaries on the Laws of Moses. From the German. 4 vols. London, 1814.

Mühlau. De Prov. Aguri et Lemuelis. Leip. 1869.

Nevius. Demon Possession and Allied Themes. By J. L. Nevius. London, 1896.

N. T. New Testament.

O. T. Old Testament.

Prym and Socin. Der neu-Aramäische Dialect des Tur 'Abdin. Von Eugen Prym u. Albert Socin.
Text u. Übersetzung. Zwei theile. Göttingen, 1881.

Renan, Ernest. History of the People of Israel. 3 vols. London, 1888—1891.

Riehm. Riehm's Handwörterbuch des Biblischen Alterthums. 2nd edition, 1894.

Roskoff. Geschichte des Teufels von Gustav Roskoff. 2 Bde. Leipzig, 1869.

Schorr. הֶחָלוּץ Wissenschaftliche Abhandlungen über Jüdische Geschichte, Litteratur u. Alterthum. Frankfort a. Maine, 1865. Heft. vii., 1872, Heft. viii.

Scholz. Götzendienst u. Zauberwesen bei den alten Hebräern. By Dr. Paul Scholz. Regensburg, 1877.

Schultz. Biblical Theology of the Old Testament. By H. Schultz. 2 vols. Edinburgh, 1893.

Schenkel. Bibel-Lexicon. By Dr. D. Schenkel, and others.

Schrader. Die Keilinscheiften u. d. alte Testament. Giessen. 2nd ed., 1883.

Scott. The Existence of Evil Spirits. By (Rev.) Walter Scott. London, 1853. (Not Sir Walter Scott, the celebrated novelist, who wrote a book on Witchcraft, &c.)

Smend. Lehrbuch der altestamentlichen Religionsgeschichte. Freibourg u. Leipzig, 1893.

Smith, W. Bible Dictionary. 2nd ed., 1894.

Smith, W. R. 1. Journal of Philology, xiii. pp. 273—288 ; xiv. pp. 113—128.
2. The Religion of the Semites. By W. Robertson Smith. Edinburgh, 1889.

Spencer. De Legibus Hebræorum ritualibus earumque rationibus. 2 vols. Tubingæ, 1732. ed. C. M. Pfaff.

Socin. Guide to Palestine. Baedeker's.

Stade. Geschichte des Volkes Israel. Von Dr. B. Stade, Berlin. 2 vols., 1887–88.

Streane. A Translation of the Treatise Chagigah from the Babylonian Talmud. By Rev. A. W. Streane, M.A. Cambridge, 1891.

Tallqvist. Die Assyrische Beschwörungserie Maqlu, &c. Von Knut L. Tallqvist. (In Acta Societatis Scientiarum Fennicæ Tomus xx., 1895.)

Tiele. Geschichte der Religion im Alterthum. Von C. P. Tiele. 1 Band. Gotha, 1896.

Tylor. Primitive Culture. 2 vols. 3rd ed. 1891.

Torreblanca. De Magia. Editio Novissima. Lugduni, 1678.

Tuch. Commentar über die Genesis. 2te Auflage, 1871.

Waite. The Occult Sciences. By Arthur Ed. Waite. London, 1891.

Weber. Jüdische Theologie. Von Dr. Terd. Weber. Zweite verbesserte Auflage. Leipzig, 1897.

Wellhausen. 1. Reste arabische Heiderstums. 2te Auflage. Berlin, 1897. 2. Isr. u. Jüd. Geschichte, 1895. 3. Die Kleinen Propheten, 1892.

Wiedemann. Religion of the Ancient Egyptians. By Alfred Wiedeman, Ph.D. London, 1897.

Winer, iii. Biblisches Realwörterbuch. Von Dr. G. B. Winer, &c. Dritte Ausgabe, 1840.

Z. A. W. Zeitschrift für die Alttestamentliche Wissenschaft. Stade.

Z. D. M. G. Zeitschrift der Deut. Morgenl. Gesellschaft.

Zimmern. Die Beschwörungstafeln Surpu. Leipzig, 1896. (Beiträge zur Kenntniss der Babylonischen Religion. Von Dr. Heinrich Zimmern. 1te Lieferung.)

MAGIC, DIVINATION, AND DEMONOLOGY

INTRODUCTION.

MAGIC, Divination, Necromancy, and Demonology are so closely connected in their character and history, that it is impossible to lay down lines between them which are fixed and exclusive.

First of all, let each be defined as clearly as may be.

DEFINITION OF MAGIC.

Magic may be briefly defined as the attempt on man's part to have intercourse with spiritual and supernatural beings, and to influence them for his benefit. It rests upon the belief so prevalent in low civilizations, that the powers in the world on which human well-being depends are controlled by spiritual agents, and that these agents are to be conciliated and made friends of by words, acts, and so forth, which are thought to please them. There is in this something analogous to religious worship and prayer. Indeed, magic and religion have many and close affinities, as will be more fully shown.[1] All magic is

---

[1] See "Magic and Religion," p. 18.

B

incipient religion, for it is an appeal to spirits believed to be more powerful and wise than man, and the methods employed to secure what is desired are no other than supplications to the goodwill of the beings consulted. Magic may be described as a low kind of religion in which the ethical element is either subordinated or sacrificed to other and inferior elements. Incantations are prayers, only that the main stress is laid on the mode of utterance rather than on the moral condition of the agent. Plants, drugs, etc., when burnt to appease the good spirits, and protect against evil ones, are to be compared with sacrifices, and especially with incense, which last obtains at the present time in many branches of the Christian Church. In the mythology of the Vedas it is hard, if not impossible, to distinguish between magical acts and sacrifices ; in each case something is done with the view of propitiating higher beings.[1]

The unethical means employed by magic correspond to the unethical view that is held of the beings trafficked with. As the conception of these beings rises, animism [2] passes through polytheism on to monotheism. At this last stage the one God believed in is just and holy, requiring on the part of all who have to do with Him moral qualifications, these above all else, these almost to the exclusion of all other qualifications. Magic has now given way to religion. Prayer and fellowship have taken the place of mere words and acts.

MAGICIANS A CLASS.

Hegel has very correctly pointed out [3] that where magic is believed in, not everyone is able or allowed to

---

[1] Hillebrandt, p. 167 f.   [2] See this term explained at p. 8 f.
[3] i. p. 281.

practise it. Special individuals are chosen on account of their superior knowledge of the formulæ, methods of operation, etc., believed to prevail with the powers which it is sought to persuade. This select body of men corresponds to the priests, which in the lower forms of religion are credited with extraordinary knowledge of Divine secrets, and with unusual influence over Deity. Indeed, it is hard to say when exactly the magician resigns, and the priest enters upon office. To some extent the conception and conduct which properly belong to magic, accompany religion in all its historical forms.[1]

Magic has been made to consist especially in the art of compelling spirits or deities, or the Deity, to do the will of him who utters the needful words, or performs the requisite acts. In this it has been made to stand apart from religion, as by d'Alviella,[2] and Professor E. Caird.[3] So also apparently Hegel,[4] but cf. p. 23 ff., "Religion and Magic." This, however, is not strictly correct, because, as already stated, all magic is a sort of religion; and certainly in most cases, the magician does not seek to use force in the exercise of his art : else what do we make of incantations and charms ?

BLACK AND WHITE MAGIC, CONJURING, NATURAL MAGIC.

In the lowest stages of culture the spirits communicated with are not separated into good and bad, just because the categories of good and bad have not risen into *conscious* thought, though implied in the very earliest thinking. Later on, traffic with evil spirits, particularly

See *intra*, p. 24. [2] See p. 87 ff. [3] i. p. 225. [4] i. p. 281.

when the purpose was to injure others, was called *Black Magic*, or the *Black Art*. *White Magic*, the contrary term, stood for intercourse with well-disposed spirits. In our own time, and amongst civilized peoples, White Magic means no more than the art of performing clever tricks with the hands, etc. Similarly the word *conjure* has, in modern English, the present meaning which White Magic has among ourselves, though originally it denotes exorcise. A *conjurer*—well, children know who he is, perhaps even better than their soberer sires. Sir David Brewster's interesting little book on "Natural Magic" gives an account of the way in which an acquaintance with the secrets of nature and of art have been used to support claims of being on intimate terms with the spiritual world. But the expression "Natural Magic" was used in this very same sense long before Sir David's time. Even Lord Bacon, in his "Advancement of Learning," has it with this signification.

Magic, Wide and Narrow Sense of.

In a narrow, but later sense, magic has to do with feats of power and not of knowledge. For this reason the relation between magic and divination has been compared to that existing between miracles and prophecy. But it will be more fully shown later on that at the beginning, and at the present among backward races, this distinction is not drawn. Indeed, divination is hardly the right word to use for what is so called at this stage, since it is really magic applied to future events. The future is not so much foretold as constituted, or made, by the art of the magician.

[1] See *infra*, p. 27.

Some Terms Explained.

The German word *zaubern* has been variously explained, but the etymology having the best support is that which connects it with the Gothic *taujan*, Old High German *zouwan* (=the modern German *thun*. Cf. English *done*). All these words mean *to do*, magic, relating to feats of power (a later and narrower sense, however, see before). Compare with these terms the Middle Latin *factura*, the Italian *fattura*, the Portuguese *feitigo* (fetish), the Spanish *hecho*, all meaning primarily something done, and secondarily magic. It was Grimm (Jacob) who first suggested the above derivation of the German word.

The English word magic is, in our language, primarily a noun, but it represents an adjective in the classical tongue, the corresponding noun for art being understood, and sometimes expressed in Latin (Ars Magica) and in Greek (μαγική τέχνη). The noun from which the classical adjective is derived is μάγος, plural μάγοι, the priestly caste among the Medes, Persians and Parthians. The root *mag* has been connected with the Indo-European root *mahâ*,[1] great, but without the slightest ground. Nor is it the Persian or Zend word denoting wise in divine things,[2] wise, excellent, priest.[3] The word came over as the thing it stood for did, from the Accadians to the Babylonians and Persians. Lenormant[4] traces the word to the Accadian *imga*, which means "respected," "honoured." Schrader[5] translates the word by *tiefandächtig* (very devout), or *tiefgelehrt* (very learned), adopting the same etymology.

Cf. Lat. *magnus*; Welsh, *mawr* (from Lat. *major*).
Porphyr., de Abstinentiâ, 4, 16.   [3] Waite, p. 11.
[4] "Chaldean Magic."   [5] p. 257.

DIVINATION

Divination may be provisionally defined [1] as the attempt on man's part to obtain from the spiritual world supernormal [2] or superhuman knowledge. This knowledge relates for the most part to the future, but it may also have to do with things in the present, such as where some hidden treasure is to be found. Divination takes for granted the primitive belief that spiritual beings exist, are approachable by man, have means of knowledge which man has not, and are willing upon certain conditions known to diviners to communicate the special knowledge which they are believed to possess.

When, as among the Israelites, divination co-existed with monotheism, or at any rate with monolatry, to use Stade's word,[3] the modes of divination were but methods of consulting deity. The Old Testament prophet, under such circumstances, differs from the diviner mainly in this, that he makes his appeal direct to God, without the employment of such means as heathen soothsayers used, which means are referred to in the Old Testament and often with approval.[4] But both diviner and prophet might, and indeed actually did, believe in Yahwe: both also sought guidance from Him.

NECROMANCY.

Necromancy is a part of divination and not a thing distinct in itself. Its peculiar mark is, that the information desired is sought from the ghosts of deceased persons. Divination embraces all attempts to obtain

---

[1] See a fuller treatment of the subject at p. 72 fr.
[2] Andrew Lang's word in his new book, " The Making of Religion."
[3] i. p. 429.   [4] See *infra*, p. 74 ff.

secret knowledge from the denizens of the spiritual world, so that necromancy comes under it, and is a part of it. Indeed, the word itself denotes literally divination (μαντεία) by consulting the dead (νεκρός).

DEMONOLOGY.

The etymology of the word demonology is no safe guide as to what the word itself means, for the Greek δαίμων denotes a supernatural being that stands midway between gods and men. He may be good or bad. Lecky says:[1] "A dæmon in the philosophy of Plato, though inferior to a deity, was not an evil spirit, and it is extremely doubtful whether the existence of evil dæmons was known to the Greeks or Romans till about the time of the advent of Christ."

We commonly understand by demonology the belief which is a part of advanced animism[2]—that there exist evil spirits which are more or less responsible for the misfortunes which assail men. In the earliest stage it is probable that good and evil spirits were not distinguished.[3] Men must from the very first have noticed in themselves and in others, dispositions and tendencies as revealed in conduct. Some men would be characterized as prevailingly good, others as prevailingly bad. I am not saying, for I do not believe, that the moral category is a merely utilitarian one, but we judge of character by acts. If it was man's thought that made him believe in the existence of innumerable beings in nature, living like himself, he must by the same process soon have divided spirits into good and bad, also resembling men.

European Morals, i. p. 404.   [2] See *infra*, p. 24.
[3] See *infra*, p. 13.

In primitive animism[1] and in the simple nature-spirit beliefs that prevailed in the midst of the Turanian tribes,[2] no hierarchy of spiritual beings can be traced. On the other hand, among the Babylonians, Assyrians, the Median Magi, and, at least in later times, among the Zoroastrians of Persia, evil spirits as well as good ones were organized into a complete system, with a supreme ruler, having under him subordinate chiefs. We meet with this developed demonology and angelology in the Old and New Testaments,[3] in the Pseudepigraphical, Apocryphal and other writings.

COMMON ORIGIN OF THE PRECEDING.

All the beliefs which have been noticed take their rise in the primitive and instinctive impulse of human beings to interpret what they see outside of themselves in terms of their own personality. The earliest knowledge which man acquires is that of himself as a living, conscious, thinking being. In a vague way he may be said to perceive the outer world as reflected in his thought before he rises to the conception of himself as standing apart from it. But surely the first *object* he knows is himself. This knowledge obtained, all other things are interpreted in its light, just as coloured glass makes what is seen through it have the same colour as itself. As man, in the wildness of unrestrained imagination, looks forth upon rivers and stars, he pictures them as living just as he is living. Have they not many of the marks of life and personality? Trees and plants stand up and apart from their environment; they also appear to eat and drink, and they produce fruit and

[1] S e *infra*, p. 9.   [2] Lenormant's "Chald. Magic," chs. xv. and xvi.
[3] See *infra*, p. 95 ff. and p. 102 ff.

beget offspring. Stones resist all efforts to move or destroy them : they often seem to move of their own accord, injuring and even killing animals and men.

"Man gazes," says Turgot, "upon the profound ocean of being, but what at first he discerns is not the bed hidden beneath its waters, but only the reflection of his own face."

It would be too much to say that at this low level ot thought the doctrine of soul as distinct from body has been reached, but it very soon is reached. In his growth to this higher thought, man is guided by his own experience. At a very early period, before there were words to suggest it, he must have come to feel that he is not the *body* : that, on the contrary, his truer selt owns and controls the body. In other words, soul is differentiated from body. This twofold view of himself is almost unthinkingly applied to other things believed to be living.

The word "animism" is used to express these primordial beliefs of man. It was first used in this connection by Dr. E. B. Tylor in a lecture delivered by him in 1867, before the Royal Society, and in the official reports of this society the lecture appears exactly as it was delivered.

The following sentences are quoted from this lecture by Mr. Herbert Spencer, and occur in a letter by him in "Literature," February 19, 1898, p. 211.

"The worship of such spirits (in general natural objects) found among the lower races over almost the whole world, is commonly known as ' fetishism.' It is clear that this child-like theory of the animation of all nature lies at the root of what we call mythology. It would probably add to the clearness of our conception of the state of mind which thus sees in all nature the action of animated life and the presence of innumerable spiritual beings, if we give it the name of animism instead of fetishism." Andrew Lang facetiously calls this kind of animism—ALL-ALIVISM.[1] But in his " Primitive Culture,"[2] chs. xi. to xvii., Dr. Tylor denotes by the term the " doctrine of souls and of spiritual beings,"[3] the existence of the latter being inferred from that of the former. This more advanced doctrine than mere ALL-ALIVISM is attained by man from his reflections upon the difference between the living and the dead, and from observations of what takes place in sleep, swoons, dreams, etc.

It has been suggested that we keep the word fetishism for that animism which regards the nature-filling spirits as inseparably joined to material objects, spiritualism doing duty for that higher kind of animism which assumes spirits to have a free and independent existence.[4] But it is a fatal objection to this last that spiritualism in English and the corresponding term in German (spiritismus) and other modern languages, has a definite meaning of a different sort, so that to make it represent also Tylor's later meaning of animism would be to make confusion worse confounded.

In this treatise I employ the term in the higher sense which it bears in Tylor's " Primitive Culture," though the other and lower kind is unquestionably more elementary and earlier in time.

Tiele mentions a stage in human culture which he alleges to be prior to animism in either of its meanings : this he calls POLYZOÏSMUS.[5] At this point man sees in

---

[1] " Literature," March 5, 1898, p. 296 .
[2] Mine is the third edition, 1891.
[3] Vol. i. p. 425 ff.
[4] Tiele, p. 6 ff.
[5] p. 8.

the world, not living beings, still less souls or spirits, but simply natural **powers** or forces. It may be said in answer to this, that the first power or force which man learns to know is that of his own personality. It is later and not earlier than he takes in the notion of natural or of any objective force. Besides, as Tiele admits,[1] there is no historical basis for his hypothesis, though he holds that it was most probably man's earliest and simplest attempt to interpret the universe in which he finds himself.[2]

The proof of animism lies in its prevalence among existing savage races, who may be considered as occupying that level of culture at which the most civilized race once was, and in the survivals among civilized nations which admit of no other explanation, e.g. magic and its allied arts, which held their ground among the ancient civilizations of Egypt, Babylonia, Greece and Rome, and of which there are traces among all the great nations or to-day. As to animism as implied in the early beliefs and practices of the Hebrews, see Stade i. 443 f. and 503 f. It is hardly needful to say that " Animism " has a different sense in the philosophy of Pythagoras (fl. B.C. 540-500 founder of the Italian school of philosophy) and in that of Plato, where it denotes the force immaterial but inseparable from matter (anima mundi) which gives the latter form and movement. Stahl, the great German chemist (*1660 : †1734), used the term to describe his theory, that all diseases have their cause in a wrong state of the soul ; their removal is therefore to be sought and secured by restoring the soul to its normal condition.

Men must at an early stage of development have reached the level of thought implied in the high animism.

[1] *Loc cit.*   [2] De la Saussaye, p. 12.

The soul is believed in dreams to forsake the body and to wander where the dreamer thinks he is. This would very naturally, Dr. Tylor considers, suggest the idea that soul and body can exist apart. Moreover, in these dreams, when the soul is supposed to be in places far removed from the body, other persons are seen as well as animals and inanimate objects in situations wholly different from those in which they are seen in waking moments, and in which persons not asleep at the time know them to be.

This mental double of human beings, of animals and of things, has been called the " apparitional soul."[1] The " apparitional soul " can be but temporarily separated as long as the individual is alive. Death gives it perfect freedom : it is under no further necessity of returning to its prison house. We find survivals of this belief in comparatively recent times.

In India, within the memory of many living men, it was the custom to bury the widow along with her deceased husband, so that her spirit might be reunited with his.

The warrior's horse was killed and interred with the body of its late master. This was done officially at Trèvres so late as 1781, though then and long before no one understood the original import of the practice. At present we do not keep up this custom, but even in our time the warrior's horse with its trappings is led to the grave, though it is not killed as formerly.

In course of time the doctrine of souls would, as Tylor points out, give rise to that of independent spirits, which had never been confined to bodies, and which were thus freer to move and to act.

[1] Tylor, i. 428.

It could not be long before these independent spirits, with which the world was peopled, were made, like men, to have not merely varying moods, some good, some bad, but permanent characters,[1] intellectual, ethical, etc. Demonology would take its rise at this point, and also angelology, if we may use this word for the belief in good spirits, a sense which the word generally carries with it in Christian Theology.

The superiority of spirit to matter must have been almost an intuition to early man. It is true that, in some respects, mind is the slave of body, and that it is made to suffer by contact not only with its own body, but also with objects around and outside, such as fire, water, air, etc. Yet, however hampered man's spirit is by its material environment, it is conscious, as matter is not; it uses matter to realize its own ends. Matter cannot sit down and form plans, using spirit as a means of carrying them out. This living, conscious, scheming, matter-controlling spirit could not but be conceived of as standing—shall I say?—head and shoulders above mere things.

Spirits that had no connection with body, that had always enjoyed this immunity, would naturally be thought of as higher than mere souls.

These again would be soon put into ranks according to their capacity and moral worth.[2] To the highest and best man would be sure to turn in the thousand and one emergencies which crowd his earthly life. Knowledge which no faculties of his could fathom, but which yet he craved for and needed : power to overcome the evil spirits that caused loss, disease, and death—these were

---

[1] See *supra*, p. 7   [2] *Supra*, p. 7.

not within his own grasp. Could this longed-for knowledge, this lacking but necessary power, be supplied by the higher spirits ?

The earliest crude endeavours to persuade these spirits to grant the knowledge and power wished for and wanted, belong to MAGIC in its primitive wide extent. (See the definition and explanation of magic.)

The deification of the most capable and honoured of these spiritual beings would follow as a natural result of the growing awe and expectation with which they were regarded.

This is not the place to either affirm or deny the existence and diffusion of a primitive revelation from God to man. The present inquiry aims at tracing the natural growth of human thought as it seems to have unfolded itself, judging by what we know of the human mind, and of the history and present condition of backward peoples.[1]

It will be seen that we are now upon the threshold of religion, if, indeed, we have not crossed it.

The following are the stages through which, according

---

[1] I wish in this note to guard myself against being misunderstood on two points. I am far from thinking that the genesis of man's knowledge of souls and of independent spirits is wholly explained by sleep, dreams, and the like. There is a prior question : how does man come to know what spirit is? this he must know before he can say or think that spirit is separable from body, is independent of body. Even to say that man's own mental experience supplies him with the notion " spirit," is to stop short of the full answer. A similar objection may be lodged against the evolution of the belief in God as supreme and absolute. But, unless the thought of God is involved in man's whole complex of thought, it could never be evolved out of it. The elaborate and interesting account given by Dr. Tylor in his epoch-making work of the steps by which man rises on his way to the conscious thought of the Infinitive and Absolute One, is, however, singularly confirmed by facts, and there is nothing in this reasoning that is contrary to the Christian idea of God or of Revelation.

to Dr. Tylor and other eminent anthropologists, man
passes in his progress to the perfect religion :—

1. Fetishism.
2. Totemism.
3. Atavism.
4. Polytheism.
5. Henotheism.
6. Monotheism.

For other classifications of positive religion, including
those of Hegel,[1] Hartmann, Tiele and Siebeck, see
De La Saussaye i. p. 11 f.

Herbert Spencer makes ancestor worship, which he
takes to be a product of dreams and of the consequent
belief in ghosts, to be the tap-root of all religion. Lyall[2]
does not go so far, for he acknowledges that euhemerism
" is not a master key which will disclose the inside of all
mythologies ; "[3] but he holds that for most of the facts,
and especially as far as India is concerned, ancestor
worship supplies an adequate explanation.

This theory fails to distinguish between the form of worship and the religious feeling itself. Ancestors are not, as
such, deities. A deeper question is, how, in any case, did
man come by the thought of God, so that ancestors or
anything else could be reverenced and adored as divine ?
Besides, we know for certain that many ancestors are not
worshipped even where, as in China and India, ancestor
worship prevails ; and it is equally certain that many
deities never were men, and got to be worshipped on
other grounds than because they were ancestors.[4]

---

[1] For Hegel's, see more fully in his " Vorlesungen über die Philosophie der Religion," i. p. 258 ff.   [2] p. 30 ff.   [3] p. 34.
[4] See Andrew Lang's answer to H. Spencer's theory in his new
book, " The Making of Religion," p. 232 ff.

MAGIC WITHOUT ANIMISM OR SUPERNATURALISM.

Dr. Tylor [1] notes a kind of magic—under which term he conforms to the primitive habit of including divination—which makes no appeal to the spirit world, and which indeed makes no acknowledgment of the existence of spiritual beings (cf. Tiele's "Polyzoïsmus"). The magician on this theory professes to have discovered the secret laws of the universe. By strong efforts of will; by traditional formulæ or rites; in short, by all the instrumentalities of magic, he causes and cures disease, inflicts misfortune or confers happiness, summons death or prevents his coming.

With an equal ignoring of spirit or God, the astrologer infers the future of human beings from the planets under which they were born. The augur makes his forecast from the movements and cries of animals and birds. The haruspice draws his conclusions from the heart or liver of slaughtered animals. Others penetrate the future from observations of thrown dice, the twitching of fingers, the tingling of ears, etc., etc.

Lyall [2] makes it to be the principal characteristic of magic that it works independently of priests and deities through supposed secret knowledge of the processes of nature. By certain words or acts the magician—whom Lyall calls the witch—claims to be able to bring about particular results. Quite inconsistently Lyall holds divination to belong to the sphere of religion. Omens, he owns, are signs supposed to be given by the gods or by God for the guidance of men. [3]

But surely these writers have gone wrong at this

---

[1] Encyc. Brit., art. Magic, cf. Prim. Cult., i. 112 f.
  p. 76 ff.   [3] p. 91.

point, for all the methods adopted in magic and in divination proceed upon the assumption that there are spiritual beings who manage the world upon regular principles, and who, upon certain conditions, deign to interfere in behalf of man. It is true that, in many instances, the consciousness of the important part played by supernatural agency is not very vivid, but it is never absent, and indeed the practices referred to have no meaning without such consciousness.

Sympathetic Magic.

What has been called "sympathetic magic,"[1] has always existed and it exists at the present time. This depends for its success largely upon the association of ideas. Its underlying assumption is that to produce any result you have but to imitate it. To burn or otherwise injure anything belonging to a person is to affect its owner in a similar way. To burn hair is to cause him to burn to whom it originally belonged. To destroy a portrait is to ruin the individual. The lover thought he softened and won the heart of his adored one by chewing and softening a piece of wood. This last is to be seen among the Zulus at the present day.

But even this could not, at the start, be anything other than a symbolic prayer to the spirit or spirits having authority in these matters. In so far as no spirit is thought of, it is a mere survival, and not magic at all, though Tylor,[2] Lyall,[3] Frazer,[4] Jevons,[5] and many others give it that name and character. I have no hesitation in saying that there has never been, and there is not at

---

[1] Jevons, p. 28 ft.   [2] i. 116 f.   [3] p. 75 ff.   [4] i. p. 9 f.
[5] p. 28 f.

the present time any magic, any divination, which has not involved and grown out of the conviction that spirits more powerful and more knowing than man, exist and can be reached by man if he uses the proper means. That so eminent a writer as Dr. Tylor misses his way in this matter is due to the fact that he is too exclusively an observer of facts, and too little the philosopher. At any rate, the predominance of man's intellectual conception of things has never taken proper hold ot Dr. Tylor. Lyall, Frazer, and Jevons are in this, as in much else, but followers of Tylor, though all are original thinkers,

MAGIC AND RELIGION.

It is difficult and, probably, impossible to draw a hard and fast line between these two. In most, if not in all positive religions there are traces or survivals of magic. In the more advanced development of magic we have the beginnings of religion.

Polytheism is the natural outgrowth of animism. The gods of polytheism are the highest and noblest spirits, and polytheism is certainly a religion. Among monotheistic peoples, nay among Christians, magical charms, amulets, etc., are exceedingly common. Note the Jewish phylacteries, mezuzas and tsitzith, and also the incantations and charms addressed to the Holy Trinity and depending for their effects upon the use of the Triune names.

A moot question is this: Is magic prior to and a stepping-stone to religion? Or, is it a step backward from religion; a corruption of religion; a belief, a practice involving a previous knowledge of religion, but a forsaking of it, or, at any rate, a rejection of religion in favour of magic?

This last opinion—that magic is a departure from religion in the strictest sense—is the old view, and among theologians it still holds the field. It is advocated by Lange,[1] Kleinert,[2] Lenormant,[3] Scholz,[4] Jevons,[5] and Lang.[6] There is no denying the fact that this view rests upon the assumption universally held by the churches until a few decades back, that all religions are due to a primitive revelation, the false ones being corruptions of the true. A recent and learned advocate, the well-known Chinese scholar, Dr. Edkins, has, within the last two or three years, written a book to support the old opinion. The title of the book is, " The Early Spread of Religious Ideas, especially in the Far East." (London, 1893.) The main argument pursued by the author is, that in matters of morals and religion the tendency of nations is, when left to themselves, to deteriorate. He instances the *Hindoos* who, in the pre-Rigveda and Rigveda stage, were monotheistic, and the Chinese who lived on a higher level of civilization and religion in the time of Confucius. But his treatment involves an enormous number of unproved and unprovable assumptions, such as, that no other causes have been at work ; that we know all the facts connected with the case, etc. Most students of anthropology and archæology, and of the science and the history of religion, and a growing number of theologians, indeed a majority of those most competent to judge, contend that at the first religion was in a very nebulous state : that, as was the case in intellectual and moral

---

[1] Herzog, Zauberei.   [2] Riehm, Zauberei.   [3] " Chald. Magic," p. 70 ff.
[4] p. 1, *et passim*. Scholz says that magic and idol worship are closely connected, and that both are departures from an original revelation of the true religion.
[5] p. 36.   [6] " The Making of Religion," p. 290.

conceptions, so likewise in religion, man's ideas advanced from lower to higher, and from higher to ever higher developments.

Religion involves purer and more advanced thought than magic. For this reason it may be expected to follow and grow out of it. History and observation of anthropological and archæological facts, survivals in folk-lore and in primitive customs—these and yet other considerations support the new view as against the old.

Jevons devotes a considerable portion of his able and interesting work to the defence and exposition of his position.

He appears to think that a belief in God, however meagre and unsatisfactory, is one element that is never absent from magic. This cannot be got until the religious stage has been reached. Therefore religion must precede magic.[1] Now we join issue with the author on this cardinal point.

Though believers in magic believe of necessity in spirits and in their superior power and skill, there is no necessity arising out of their magic, that they should contemplate these spirits as divine. Magic does not involve more than the superiority indicated above : it has existed and now exists in cases where the category of deity has never been attained unto.

It is contended further, that religion has never been known, as a matter of fact, to arise out of magic ; but that on the contrary, the decay of religion has been generally accompanied by the adoption of magic. The Old Testament is referred to as indicating the purity of the

[1] Cf. with this Sir Max Müller's contention (Hibbert Lectures) that fetishism is a declension from a higher religion, since it involves the idea of deity, of the infinite.

early religion of Israel. The implicit, and even explicit magical teaching in the Talmud,[1] the mysticism and theosophy, the theurgic doctrines of the Jewish Qabbalah show us Israel's religion in its later and corrupter state.

Christianity judged by its earliest literature—New Testament, etc., gives no countenance to the vagaries of magic and divination. But some of the most eminent Qabbalists were like Reuchlin († 1592), Christian scholars, who saw in the curious and ingenious mysteries of the Qabbalah the Trinity, the Atonement, and all the central verities of the Christian faith. In the Middle Ages witches were condemned and executed, not because they had no power over nature and men, but because they had such power and exercised it to the detriment of others.

Martin Luther spoke thus of the witches who in his day spoiled a farmer's butter and eggs, " I would have no pity on those witches, I would burn them all."

In Scotland and in Germany, until comparatively recent times, Roman Catholic priests were believed to have magical power. In cases of emergency it was not an uncommon thing for Protestant clergymen in these countries to consult their Roman Catholic rivals. (See Tylor's " Primitive Culture,[3]" i. 115 ff.)

The same feature appears to characterize Islam. There is not a word in the Quran which countenances magic. On the contrary, see Surah ii. 96, ٱلشَّيَاطِينُ يُعَلِّمُونَ ٱلنَّاسَ ٱلسِّحْرَ " The Satans taught men magic." Similarly in the Traditions—Mishkât—(Book xxi., ch. 3, part i.) magic is censured. Yet the recorded sayings of Mohammed permit practices that are closely akin to magic. See examples in Hughes' " Dictionary of Islam," p. 303b. f.

---

[1] See *infra*, p. 61 ff.

Nevertheless it is true that in subsequent times Islam became more and more addicted to magic. Many are the zealous Moslems who have devoted themselves to the secret arts.

In regard to divination the course seems to have been different. Mohammed did not claim the power of divining, yet he often availed himself of the services of the Qahin الكاهن, who did claim to possess and exercise this power. After the prophet's death many arose who pretended to be Allah's authorized exponents of the faith, who said they were in this the successors of Mohammed. Among these were Maslama, Tulhaiha, al-Alwa. But it was soon pointed out that the Quran and the traditions (sunna) supplied all the guidance that was needed.[1] It is impossible not to be reminded by this explanation of the uselessness of magic, of the parallel argument adduced in Deut. xviii. 10 f. Yet there is a difference. The Israelites are to keep far away from magic and divination, for God now speaks to them in the prophets. Mohammed himself was the prophet: his words, his instruction, were preserved in the Quran and the Sunnat, and nothing further was wanted.

There are very few instances, and none that are conclusive, to show that magic denotes a devolution from the religious stage.

There are many peoples in all the great continents who very largely practise magic, but who have never risen above the lowest fetishism, which indeed may be called a kind of religion, though it is not the kind of religion which Jevons and his school have in mind.

On the other hand, among the advocates of the view

---

[1] Wellh. Reste, 137 f.

that religion is evolved out of magic stand the names of Tiele and of the celebrated German philosopher, Hegel († 1831). In his "Vorlesungen über die Philosophie der Religion," Hegel deals with the subject under consideration. To understand his position it is needful to have a clear view of his theory of knowledge.

Man is first of all conscious of what is called the objective, though it is an objective in thought, and not in any world which lies outside of thought. In this objective consciousness there is involved the knowledge of himself as the subject who is thus conscious, and of the absolute unity through which subject and object are brought into relation. In the beginning it is the objects around man that strike him, and which indeed constitute for him the only realities. He is dependent upon them, and has to make with them the best terms he can. Hegel called religion which can under these conditions exist, "immediate natural religion[1]": immediate, because the things seen are treated as the whole of what exist, just as the dreamer takes what he sees in his dream to be the only realities. This kind of religion is to be compared with fetishism, in which the object is the sole thing worshipped, or at least in which subject and object are one. This is the lowest form of magic. Strictly speaking, man can, according to Hegel, be truly religious then only when he has risen to the consciousness of himself as distinct from the not self, and when he feels himself a free man, and as such, master over nature, or, at any rate, able to control the powers of nature by exercising the right means.[2] First of all, the magician seeks to influence nature, or rather the spirits of nature

---

[1] i. 263.   [2] i. 281.

directly, by word of mouth, or by gesture. At higher levels of civilization means are employed, such as sacrifices, etc., for the beings dealt with have now to be appeased, persuaded, etc., by gifts and the like.

The full religious experience, however, is enjoyed only after man has risen to the full conception of God as absolute and perfect. But this higher knowledge is involved, and, to some extent, actually realized in the lowest objective mental acts. That is to say, magic in its crudest form involves religion in its purest, and is, in fact, on the way to being the perfect religion.

Dr. Tylor [1] writes thus :—

"Magic belongs in its main principles to the lowest stages of civilization, and the lower races, who have not partaken largely of the education of the world, still maintain it in vigour."

In his Encyclopædia article he says that in low stages of civilization magic and religion are hardly distinguished : the sorcerer [2] is also the priest. This view was long ago advocated by Meiners.[3]

The true state of the case appears to be this,—

1. Magic, as the non-ethical attempt of man to influence the supernatural, may be said to accompany all grades of religion ; Christianity itself, in all its actual forms, is more or less influenced by it.

2. Since magic is a low form of religion, it may either precede the full realization of religion, or it may follow upon this last, and so be, in that case, a degeneration, a going back from religion. I do not think that Hegel

---

[1] Prim. Cult., i. 112.

[2] By which he means the man who is magician and diviner ; but the sorcerer is, strictly speaking, a diviner.

[3] "Geschichte aller Religionen," book xii. M. was a professor at Göttingen ; † 1810.

would have had anything to say against this presentation, since his development is not necessarily always forward : it indicates rather different degrees of perfection which with continuous progress, will be reached : it is the progress of the tide rather than that of the dawn : in the main, however, there is literally progress.

MAGIC AND SCIENCE.

It has been often pointed out that magic is science in the making, just as it has been said to be religion in the making. Thus Jevons[1] shows that savage logic goes upon all fours with the logic of, say, John Stuart Mill. The same methods are followed—agreement, difference, concomitant variations, etc., in coming to conclusions regarding the future. Sympathetic magic he holds to be simply a case of the same mode of reasoning. But Jevons himself admits that the belief in the uniformity of nature which lies at the bottom of primitive man's logic, rests upon the previous belief that there are in all nature indwelling spirits. The logic is a corollary deduced from the spirit-belief.

Magic has been in a special manner compared with early medical science. Incantations, plants, and amulets have a scientific aspect. Incantations have an efficacy in soothing nervous patients. Plants and other physical agents have, in certain cases, definite remedial effects, and they are thus described as having the power of casting out devils, just because they heal the diseases believed to be due to demon possession. In course o time incantations and the use of material things (either as solids, liquids or odours), came to be regulated

[1] Ch. iv.

on sanitary principles ; but it must not be forgotten that at first these things had a religious significance, and that alone.

We have an analogous process of religious usage passing into science in the distinction found in the Old Testament and in other religions, between clean and unclean food. J. D. Michaelis[1] and others hold that this distinction originated in health considerations. In a paper on " The Health Laws of the Bible," read at the 1891 Oriental Congress,[2] Mr. Marcus N. Adler, M.A., F.S.S., strongly supports this view ; nor does he seem to know that any other explanation has been ever put forward.

The study of comparative religion and especially that of the religion of the Semites, has placed the matter beyond the possibility of doubt that clean and unclean, when applied to food, were in the first instance, religious conceptions, as is maintained by Dillmann,[3] Stade,[4] Wellhausen, W. Robertson Smith,[5] F. B. Jevons,[6] and most recent scholars. Whatever among primitive peoples had to do with the gods, if, for example, they were totem plants or animals, were as such, taboo or prohibited as food. It is almost amusing to think that unclean and holy have a common origin, and at the start denote the same thing, viz. that which was taboo. Thus W. R. Smith says[7] : " Holy and unclean things have this in common, that in both cases certain restrictions lie on men's use of and contact with them, and that the breach of these restrictions involves supernatural dangers."

[1] Vol. iii. p. 219 ff.
[2] Published in the *Asiatic Quarterly* for January, 1892.
[3] On Leviticus xi.   [4] i. p. 48 ff.
[5] Rel. Sem., 143 ff., and 427 ff.
[6] Rel. Sem., p. 62, *et passim*.   [7] Rel. Sem., p. 427.

Yet what originated in religious superstition is often rationalized, so that further regulations proceed upon scientific principles ; so much so that the religious origin is forgotten and even denied. Religion in the early form of magic or in some higher form, has given rise to nearly all our science, and to very much of our art. Even poetry, music, sculpture, and pastimes like dancing, received their first suggestion and earliest impetus in the religious sphere. Only in the modified sense, demanded by what has now been said, is it true that magic is elementary science, or science in the process of being born.

MAGIC AND DIVINATION.

Among the least advanced races, and in the lowest levels at which civilized nations have been, no distinction is drawn between magic and divination. W. Robertson Smith[1] says that it was in the decadence of the old religions that these two tended to run into one another. He instances the Greeks as a nation which legalized divination and yet condemned magic as a black art. He might have added the Egyptians and Romans as other examples.

But both history and philosophy are against him. Differentiation is the mark of a late and not of an early time. Both magic and divination come under the category of intercourse with the spirit world ; whether the aim be to acquire secret knowledge or superhuman power, the proceeding was at first similar.

To obtain a message from the other world, such as a

[1] Journal of Phil., xiv. p. 121 .

prophetic dream, the ancient Egyptians took a black cat which had been killed, and wrote on a tablet with a solution of myrrh, a certain incantation in which the name of the god to be invoked was mentioned. This tablet was to be placed in the cat's mouth. The dream came, with the desired intimation. (See Wiedemann's "Religion of the Ancient Egyptians," Eng. Ed. 1897, p. 267 f.) Now, here the methods of magic are employed to gain the ends of divination. Both are, in fact, united in the same process. In the Biblical נָחָשׁ I am inclined to see an appeal to the serpent god, the appeal being made by magical means. (But see under this word.)

In Torreblanca's book " De Magia," the writer divides his subject thus :—

I. *De Magia Divinatrice.*

II. *De Magia Operatrice.*

So careful a writer as Dr. Tylor uses language which makes magic include divination.[1]

It will be presently pointed out that in the Old Testament magic and divination often go together under one designation, e.g. קֶסֶם etc.

Nevertheless, there are obvious advantages in considering the two apart as Robertson Smith does. But it should constantly be kept in mind that at first the two were not differentiated, and that in all ages, including our own, magic is made to do duty for both.

MAGIC AND DEMONOLOGY.

At the first, as at present among savage peoples, the spirits communicated with were not sharply distinguished

---

[1] See Prim. Cult., i. 134.

as good and bad. Since magic in the narrow sense tends more and more to have the character of constraint, it being sought by means of drugs, by forms of words, etc., to force the evil spirit by means of the good one ; therefore more and more magic got to be associated with evil spirits.

I have already alluded[1] to the distinction made in later times between so-called "Black" and "White" magic. The distinction was not originally made, because good and evil spirits were not separated in thought, though the separation, and, indeed, the opposition of the two classes, must soon have occurred to reflecting human beings.

It will be seen in the course of this essay how impossible it is to keep magic and demonology apart. The methods adopted to ward off demons or to prevent their evil influences are magical, and this is the kind of magic of which we have far more traces than of any other among the Hebrews and among all nations ancient and modern.

[1] See *supra*, p. 3 .

I. MAGIC.

MAGIC IN THE OLD TESTAMENT.

Traces and Survivals.

OF the early history of the Hebrews we have little knowledge that is certain. The most ancient portions of the Old Testament belong, at least as literature, to the period between B.C. 800 and B.C. 900. Neither J nor E can be pushed further back than the last date, and Dillmann even does not claim for E (his B) a remoter origin than B.C. 850. J (his C) is a century younger.

Wellhausen and his school exactly reverse these dates, making J the older. The traditions contained in these documents may be very much older than the documents themselves. That they must be older goes without saying, but how much it is impossible to say.

Wellhausen begins his "Geschichte des Israels" with Moses. Before him we are in the realm of uncertainty. Even as to what Moses did and said we are much in the dark, though that he was humanly the founder of the nation, as such, and of its religion, there is no doubt; Wellhausen himself admitting this much.

But the religion of Israel for a long time after the kingdom was founded was polytheistic in this sense, that the nation and its leaders believed as much in the existence of other gods as in that of Yahwe. But for *them* there was but one God ; Him alone they were to worship, and in return He would protect them against their foes and against the deities whom their foes rightly worshipped. Stade[1] calls this belief of Israel " monolatry," as distinct from monotheism ; by Pfleiderer it is called " henotheism," a term so variously understood that De La Saussaye rightly advises its being given up.

How the belief in Yahwe's absoluteness, uniqueness and universal dominion arose, is admirably sketched by Riehmi in his " Messianische Weissagungen " (Messianic Prophecy).[2]

If, of course, the Genesis account, or rather accounts[3] of Creation be accepted, as they used to be, and as in some quarters they still are, as the very work of Moses, then Israel's religion was from its historical beginning monotheistic. Nearly all Old Testament scholars, however, now agree that both accounts are of much more recent origin, the principal one not being older than the Exile, nor perhaps so old. This last, the P narrative, is probably based on the Babylonian cosmologies, with which Israel during the Exile must have become familiar, though it is edited and adapted to the belief in one God, the Creator and Preserver of all.

What were the beliefs and practices of Israel before the historical period, which Wellhausen makes to start with Moses, it is hard, nay impossible, positively to say.

But this is noteworthy that from the very earliest period at which we find the Hebrews, their attitude

---

[1] i. 429.   [2] p, 92 *et passim* (English, 2nd edition).
[3] Gen. i.—ii. 4a (P), and ii. 4b—23 (J).

towards magic and related practices was almost wholly negative and hostile.

The late Rabbi David Joel (" Aberglaube " etc.) goes much further than facts justify him in making the Old Testament Hebrews wholly innocent of the black art. He is not able to make so complete a vindication of the Tannaim, or authors of the Mishna, but he holds that on the whole they stand in the same hostile position towards magic that the Bible writers do. He is able to maintain his position only by forcing meanings upon the Old Testament and upon the Mishna, which the texts will not allow.

He connects magic with a belief in demons, and says it implies a seeking unto them instead of unto Yahwe. He affirms that there is no belief in devils in the books of Moses. עֲזָאזֵל (Azazel, Lev. xvi. 8, 10, 26) is no demon, but a steep mountain as the Talmud said before. שֵׁדִים (shēdim), in Deut. xxxii. 17, are not demons, but simply lords or gods.

The Teraphim of Rachel show that she had not quite cut herself off from heathenism ; but they have no countenance in Genesis.

When Balaam was made to bless instead of cursing Israel as he intended, there is no acknowledgment of his having any real power to influence the people either by blessing or cursing. God wrought a miracle and compelled Balaam to bless the very people he was sent to curse; and the purpose of this miracle was to show that the pretensions of Balaam were null and void. Yet to an impartial reader the narrative in Num. xxii.— xxiv., implies on the part of the writer a recognition of the claims put forth by Balaam, just as Exodus vii. 8 ff.

contain a tacit acknowledgment that the magicians of Egypt had supernormal or supernatural power—they as truly as Moses, though not to the same extent. Compare with both these the attitude of Christian people up to a comparatively recent time.[1]

Goldziher[2] has shown that among the ancient Arabs as among the Jews, the magical word of blessing and of cursing played a prominent part. In war, the poet, by cursing the enemy rendered service not second to the warrior himself. The word uttered was, in fact, a most potent "fetish," as Goldziher has it.[3] The Jews of Medina brought into their synagogues images of their archfoe Malik b. al-Aglam; and at these they hurled curses every time they came together. In the light of what Goldziher says, there is no denying the magical character assumed by Balaam, and it is equally clear that the reality of the power claimed is acknowledged in the Bible narrative. Else why seek to transfer his services to the cause of Israel?

I may add that the Balaam incident occurs in the oldest document of the Hexateuch, that known as the Jehovistic and designated by J E. The Exodus account of the plagues and the magicians is taken from P, and is therefore much later.

Besides what Goldziher has written, Brinton,[4] Hillebrandt[5] and others, have also shown the wide prevalence of the belief in the potency of the uttered word. Cf. "Curse ye me Meroz," of Deborah's song in Judges v. 23 (date, time of the Judges).

The evil eye, Joel will have it, has nothing in it that is mystical or magical; it means in the Bible, the

---

[1] See *supra*, p. 23.   [2] p. 26 ff.   [3] p. 28.
[4] p. 88 ff.   [5] p. 169 ff.

D

Mishna, etc., simply envy. He does not seem to have followed the history of this superstition.[1]

In a similar manner he (Dr. J.) makes strenuous efforts to clear the authorities of the Mishna from complicity in the black art.

It is nevertheless true that the attitude of the Old Testament is, on the whole, unfavourable to magic. This is very remarkable when it is remembered how given to this superstition the surrounding nations were.

There are not wanting, however, instances of practices magical in origin, and having no other real significance, though in later times other explanations have been supplied. I must refer for some of these to my discussion of Demonology in the Old Testament, page 95 ff. But here I want to refer to one or two special cases.

Gen. xxx. 14 (J). Leah wanted more children. Her son Reuben goes into the field and brings her דּוּדָאִים (dudaim) or "mandrakes," fruit growing on plants of the Belladonna kind, having white and red strong-smelling flowers. Cf. Cant. vii. 14. This plant, called by naturalists *Mandragora vernalis*, though there is also a *Mandragora autumnalis*, is common enough in Palestine, and especially in Galilee. Its fruit was supposed to have the power of awakening sexual feeling and of promoting fertility. Among the Arabs the يَبْرُوح (yabruḥ) was believed to have the same effect, and is almost certainly the same fruit. W. R. Smith ("Rel. Sem.," p. 423) says the mandrake, known as Baaras among the Northern Semites, was supposed by the Arabs and by the ancient Germans to be inhabited by a spirit which gave it extraordinary powers. Many Arab stories told of the

---

[1] See "The Evil," by Ellworthy.

Yabruḥ confirm this. The Hebrew word is undoubtedly derived from the root דּוּד (dud), which means "to love," דּוֹד (dōd), beloved (friend). On דּוּדָאִים (dudaim) as love potions, see Tuch on this passage.[1]

Now, in this early part of the Old Testament (it belongs to J), we have effects ascribed to this fruit which could not be supposed to follow from its natural properties : either it frustrated the work of the demon that caused sterility, or it had some peculiar influence upon the spirit of good. And not one syllable of disapproval is expressed by the Redactor who incorporated J into his work.

I am not sure whether another incident recorded in the same chapter and belonging to the same source (J) is not to be reckoned in the category of magic, though it would be magic of the sympathetic or symbolic kind. The peeled rods which Jacob put in front of the sheep and goats as they came to drink water, caused those that were pregnant to bring forth young that were spotted and striped. The natural explanation may be adequate, but it is probable that more than this was in the mind of the writer.

There is a good deal of uncertainty as to the Teraphim which Rachel stole when she and Jacob left her father's house, Gen. xxxi. 19 ff. They were of human form (1 Sam. xix. 13), and were looked upon as gods (v. 30 and Judges xviii. 24), though their possession is regarded as illegitimate (Josiah put them away together with the wizards, etc., 2 Kings xxiii. 24 ; cf. Zech. x. 2, where they are associated with diviners).

Among the Assyrians, images of gods were kept in the house because they were believed to have the power

Cf. Lang's "Custom and Myth," p. 143 ff.

of warding off evil spirits.   A certain exorcist is said to
have had statues of the gods Lugalgirra and Allamu put
one on each side of the main entrance to his house, and
in consequence he felt perfectly impregnable against all
evil spirits.   (See Tallq. p. 22.)

It is probable that in Genesis and elsewhere we should
construe the word as plural of excellence or of majesty,
answering to אֱלֹהִים, אֲדוֹנִים, קָדֹשִׁים (see Gesenius [20]
§124, g).   The root is generally believed to be the same
as the Arabic ترف (tarifa), which means to live a life of
ease and plenty.   The Teraphim was kept in the house
as a guarantee of good luck.   Though originally perhaps
an idol, it was afterwards and in Biblical times almost
exclusively a kind of charm.[1]   That it had a magical
import is suggested by Zech. x. 2, where Teraphim,
diviners, and " tellers of false dreams " are put in the
same category.   The use of Teraphim was not always
condemned, as is proved by this Genesis narrative, for
nothing is said by Jacob or the writer (J), or the Redactor
that is disparaging: and by Hos. iii. 4, where it is said that
on account of her disloyalty Israel shall be for many days
" without king, without prince and without sacrifice, and
without pillar and without ephod or teraphim."

Baudissen ("Studien," etc., i. 57) sees in the worship
of Teraphim a proof of the original polytheism of the
Israelites ; these idols—with him the word is strictly
plural—holding a lower place in the esteem of the people
than Jehovah, similar to that assigned saints in Catholic
popular belief (" katholischen Volksglauben ").

In the prohibition, " Thou shalt not seethe a kid in
its mother's milk " (Ex. xxiii. 19, xxxiv. 26; Deut. xiv. 21),

---

[1] Cf. Lares and Penates, the household gods of the Romans.

Maimonides, Abarbarnel, Nic. de Lyra, and an anonymous Qaraite commentator, followed by Spencer, and other more modern scholars have seen an allusion to a magical broth which was sprinkled over trees, plants, and fields, in order to make them fertile the following year. Such a custom prevailed among the Zabians and other Eastern peoples. (See Spencer, i. 335 ff.) It is more likely that we have in the words a reference to an ancient form of sacrifice, similar to the sacrifice of blood (Smith, W. R., Rel. Sem. p. 203, note 8).

In Isaiah iii. 2, among the stays and supports which would be taken from the nation in consequence of their sin are named: the mighty man גִּבּוֹר, the man of war אִישׁ מִלְחָמָה, the judge שׁוֹפֵט, the prophet נָבִיא, the diviner קֹסֵם, and the elder זָקֵן. The connection in which the word occurs would seem to imply that קֹסֵם was a permitted and irreproachable functionary. He is mentioned among the elite of the land.

Exodus vii. and viii. is in this connection interesting, for in these chapters the miracle-working power of the magicians חַרְטֻמִּים is acknowledged in the narrative. Aaron's rod becomes a serpent, so do the rods of the magicians. Aaron's power is indicated as greater than theirs, for his rod swallows theirs (vii. 11 f.). Aaron turned the waters into blood, so did his rivals (vii. 22). He caused the land to abound with frogs, so did they (viii. 3). The plague of stinging flies[1] which Aaron caused to come, the magicians failed to produce (viii. 18). It is noteworthy that all these acknowledgments of the power of the magicians are due to P; this is more striking, as much of the connected narrative is due to

---

[1] כִּנִּים (kinnim): A.V. and R.V., "lice."

older sources (J, JE, R). We may have in this tacit acknowledgment of the reality of magic, an effect of the residence in Babylon. As, however, the same word (חַרְטֻמִּים, khartummim) occurs in a much older source, (E, Gen. xli. 8, 24) to describe the magicians whom Pharaoh called to interpret his dream, it is most likely that the writer (P) borrowed from E. He would be the more easily led thereto, as the events in both cases transpired in Egypt.

One great reason which induced the Hebrews to condemn magic and the like was that it was so closely connected with idolatry. In 2 Kings ix. 22 it seems identified with it.

To the Hebrews, deities worshipped by other peoples were evil spirits or demons with which magicians and diviners were supposed to traffic. To practise magic and divination or to support them meant to them—at least to the pious orthodox among them—an acknowledgment of idols. It is significant of this that Hebrew names for heathen gods found in the Old Testament,[1] have been translated in many cases in the Septuagint by " demons."[2] In a similar way the Jinns, or demons of Islâm were, in the "times of ignorance," gods worshipped as such : e.g., قُزَح (Quzah).[3] The Romans also looked upon the gods of other nations as demons, and as hostile to themselves and to the deities they worshipped.[4]

In Samuel vi. we have an example of what has been called symbolic magic. The Philistines, after conquering the Israelites at Aphek, take from the latter the Ark which they place in the temple of Dagon. The god falls

---

[1] אֱלִילִים, שֵׁדִים, etc.   [2] δαιμόνια.
[3] See *infra*, p. 121.   [4] Dr. Granger, p. 174.

to pieces in the presence of the Ark, and besides, the people are afflicted with tumours [A.V., emerods(= hemorrhoids)] and the land covered with mice. They resolve to send back the Ark to the Israelites, but following the directions of their priests, they fill the Ark with golden images of the tumours and mice. By means of these last they expected to get rid of their tormentors. Some causal connection was believed to exist between the golden images and the originals. They might, of course, have been regarded as offerings to God, made that He might be induced to stay the pests. In favour of this was the custom among heathen nations of hanging in temples, images of parts of the body which had been healed [1] as indicating the gratitude of the persons restored to health. But the fact of the resemblance between the evil and the means used to remove it supports the view that the images were thought in some way to have the power of removing that which they were images of. Among the Dacotahs in North America at the present time, when anyone is ill, an image of his disease—a boil or what not—is carved in wood. This little image is then placed in a bowl of water and shot at with a gun. The image of the disease being destroyed, the disease itself is expected to disappear." [2]

The golden serpent erected by Moses so that those who had been bitten by the fiery serpents might, by looking at it, be healed [3] is a remnant of the same practice. By gazing at the golden image of the serpent, the bites of the live serpents were cured. It need not surprise anyone who believes that, in this particular case, Divine

[1] See Classical references in Winer's R. Wb³. ii. 255.
[2] Andrew Lang, " Myth, Ritual, and Religion," i. 98.
[3] Num. xxi. 6-9.

power was really put forth, for how often does God accommodate both speech and action to the conceptions and habits of those whom He deals with !

BIBLICAL TERMS.

The most able, recent, and helpful treatment of the greater number of words or expressions employed in the Old Testament in connection with magic, divination, and demonology, is contained in the two articles written by the late Dr. W. R. Smith for the " Journal of Philology." Since he examines those only which occur in Deut. xviii. 10, 11, his treatment is not, of course, complete for the Old Testament ; and it does not pretend to touch the New Testament, and, as a matter of fact, it does not.

There is another drawback in Dr. Smith's subtle and learned discussion. Following a hint dropped by Ewald [2] that the above verses contained a summary of the " worst kinds of divination (and magic ?) current at the time of the author," and that the arrangement is intentional, he is too anxious to get out and establish certain meanings which put the words and phrases into a definite relation to another. This will appear further on.

OLD TESTAMENT TERMS.

Some of the terms embrace the idea of divination as well as that of magic, which ought to create no surprise as the ideas are so closely connected.

---

[1] xiii. 273-288, xiv. 113-128.

[2] " Lehre der Bibel von Gott," i. 230. See translation of the passage at p. 214 of " Revelation ; its Nature and Record," being translation, with some omissions, of vol. i. of Ewald's work. The translation is by my able predecessor, the late Principal Goadby, B.A., who passed suddenly away in 1889, to everyone's sorrow who knew him, just as his best work was about to be done.

Two words appear to have had originally no exclusive reference to either divination or magic. One of these is חֲכָמִים (khakamim ; Aram. חַכִּימִים ; LXX., σόφοι, σοφισταὶ) ; it denotes literally "wise men." In Ex. vii. 11 they are named alongside of the מְכַשְּׁפִים (mekash-shephim), or magicians, the latter word being used, I think, to explain the first ; the writer wishes to make it clear what kind of " wise men " he means, hence he adds the specific term to the generic.

In the next clause the word חַרְטֻמִּים (khartummim) stands for the same individuals. This word I regard also as generic.[1]

Lenormant[2] thinks a special class of magicians is meant, viz. those who used magic to cure diseases ; but he is evidently led away in this notion by the Arabic word حَكِيم (ḥakeem), which in the modern speech has the special meaning of physician. طَبِيب (ṭabeeb) is, however, the commoner word.

The second chapter of Daniel seems to supply a key to the meaning of the term. In verse 12 we are told that Nebuchadnezzar the king gave orders that all the *wise men* were to be put to death, because they had failed to interpret his dream. *Who* were those that were commanded to tell the king his dream ? They were (v. 2) the magicians חַרְטֻמִּים (khartummim), a general term for the enchanters אַשָּׁפִים (ashshaphim), the sorcerers מְכַשְּׁפִים (mekashshephim), and the Chaldeans כַּשְׂדִּים (kasdim).

In v. 48 we read that God made Daniel to be head over all the *wise men ;* i.e. clearly all spoken of in verse 2.

---

[1] See *infra*, p. 42 ᴵ. [2] "Chald. Magic," p. 14.

חַרְטֻמִּים (khartummim) is another word of general import. Of its etymology the opinion used to be, and it still generally prevails, that the word has as its basis חֶרֶט (kheret), a chisel to cut with—as stone (Exod. xxxii. 4), a sharp metallic instrument to write with; then, as in Isaiah viii. 1, the stylus with which one writes. חַרְטֻמִּים (khart.) would then mean the scribes, the learned class, a meaning closely connected with חֲכָמִים (khakamim). Both Ewald and Dillmann contend for this derivation.

We have in Assyrian a noun *khiritu*, a place dug, a grave, ditch, canal; but the t represents ת not ט; and moreover it is a servile, not a radical, as the form from which it comes is Kharu or Khiru (חרה).

Hoffmann (Z. A. W., iii. p. 89, f.), followed by Sigfried, makes خَلْم (khatmun) (*nose*) the root, the ח being thus designated because they spoke in a low nasal tone; cf. Robertson Smith's derivation of מְעוֹנֵן (me'onen) from غَنّ (ghanna), to emit a hoarse, nasal sound; cf. also the Greek γοήτες (2 Tim. iii. 13), men who used a low, mournful voice, then magicians.

If, however, we are to accept a Semitic origin for the word, the first derivation is more likely, as the root in that case actually exists in Hebrew. The termination ōm (=ām, cf. Stade, § 77a) is common in Hebrew: cf. דָּרוֹם, גִּדְעֹם, פִּדְיֹם. (See Stade, § 295.) If the Arabic root be accepted, we have the ר (resh) inserted instead of dag. forte, as is common in Aramaic (כֻּרְסָא), Arabic كُرْسِيّ, Hebrew כָּרְסֵם, and Ethiopic.

It is not at all improbable that E got the word from Egypt, and that we are to seek its origin in the Egyptian language. It occurs first of all in Gen. xli. 8, 24, the source being E. It then occurs in Exod. vii. 9, the source being P. Its third and only remaining occurrence is in Dan., a book written some time in the first half of the second century B.C.

In Genesis it stands for dream interpreters, i.e. diviners. In Exodus it is used for those who wrought the same miracles as Aaron—turning rods into serpents, etc. Remembering that magic in the modern narrow sense was not anciently separated from divination, it is surely not too much to say that the word חֹר in Gen. and Exod. is a general one. The LXX. renders variously by ἐξηγηταί (expounders), ἐπαοιδοί (chanters—those who say the incantations), and φαρμακοί (those who use drugs for magical ends), a proof that these translators were as uncertain as we are as to what exactly the word signifies.

Lenormant (" Chald. Magic ") says the word means exorcists, those who cast out evil spirits, but he gives no reason.

Daniel was, we have seen, made President of the wise men (חֲכִימִים) (Dan. ii. 48). In Dan. iv. 6 we are told he was made head of the חַרְטֻמִּים (khartummim). It need not affect our position that in v. 11 he was made chief of the גָזְלִין, כַּשְׂדָּאִין, אָשְׁפִין, חַרְטֻמִּים. The first word is really what the writer means, the rest are mere interpretations or specifications of this one; just as in Ex. vii. 11, מְכַשְּׁפִים (mekashshephim) is an interpretation of the word it follows. It is possible that in both cases the words which come after are glosses added by a later hand.

I take it then that both חֲכִימִין and חַרְטֻמִּים are general terms. The last is the older word, and it may be either Egyptian or a loan word used by the Egyptians. At any rate, there is no good reason for saying that it is Babylonian, as it occurs in the E document. חַבִּימִין is probably got from Babylon, and may be the Semitic rendering of the Accadian *emga*, or the Persian مغ (*magh*).

OLD TESTAMENT WORDS FOR MAGIC OR IN RELATION TO IT.

Now let us come to words which are more specific. I begin with that word for magic which is most general and which is used even more for divination.

1. קֶסֶם (qesem). I place this among words for magic because I think that primarily it had that sense, though the secondary meaning, when it got way, outstripped and almost shut out the primary.

Fleischer[1] and Mühlau u. Volck[2] maintain the primary magical meaning of this word. W. R. Smith[3] is so sure that the contrary opinion is right, that but " for the great name of Fleischer it would be hardly necessary to waste a word on the rival theory that the word first meant a magical formula and then came to denote divination."

Wellhausen[4] writes equally strongly against Fleischer's etymology. He says, " Das ist speculative Etymologie alten Stils, die auf das Verfahren bei der Sache keine Rücksicht nimmt und sich um die sogenannten Antiquitäten nicht kümmert." While Robertson Smith makes " decision " the fundamental thought in the word, Wellhausen thinks it is " allotment or distribution " (Zutheilung). Stade[5] follows Smith and Wellhausen as against Fleischer.

---

[1] Quoted by Delitzsch on Isa. iii. 2.   [2] Gesenius's Lex.[10]
[3] Jour. Phil., xiii. 279.   [4] Reste, p. 134.   [5] i. 503, note

In proof of his general position, R. Smith seeks confirmation from the Arabic. In Quran v. 4 we have the phrase استقسام بالازلم obtaining a divine decree at the Sanctuary by headless arrows.

Rodwell renders this phrase "division of the slain by consulting arrows," but it probably means seeking an oracle by arrows according to an ancient custom of mixing arrows and letting one be taken out at random. Rodwell refers to the classical passage in Pockock,[1] and this might, if carefully read, have guided him to a better interpretation.

W. R. Smith supplies other references to Arabic writers to show that the word means to consult the deity or deities by drawing lots. But that the word did have this secondary meaning no scholar, and least of all Fleischer, would doubt. The question is : What is its *primary* meaning ?

The story he gives on p. 219 from Bokhārī, iv. 219 f., headed in the original, "The qasama in the time of heathenism," tells more against Smith's theory than for it. The oath was resorted to in order to find out who was guilty of a particular murder. The tribe charged with the crime take an oath of innocence, and soon all die. Now the appeal is by oath. But this oath is simply a kind of magical conjuration ; had it been true and correct it could have influenced the deities appealed to in a contrary direction. It is a case of magical language and methods brought into the service of divination. Or, better still, at the beginning the two were not distinguished, both being regarded as appeals to spirits or gods. He refers for Biblical usage to

[1] "Specimen." Ed. White, p. 318.

Prov. xvi. 16, where the word is used, with no colouring, of a king's decision ; to Ezek. xxi. 22, where the king of Babylon shot his arrows in order to know which of two ways to take.

Rashi on Deut. xviii. 10, explains the קוֹסֵם as one who divines by a rod. He refers to Hosea iv. 12 for a parallel instance (Greek ῥαβδομαντεία).

From this primary meaning of divining by lot the word acquired the general meaning of decision, giving sentence, the קוֹסֵם being one who seeks such a decision. Its commonest rendering in the LXX., μαντὶς, shows its wider connotation.

W. R. Smith proceeds to show from Aramaic usage that قُوصِفا is the most general word for revealer, diviner, among the heathen Arameans, though proofs of the narrow sense—divination by lot—are not wanting. Assuming the view of W. R. Smith, קסם to cut, may be explained by the cutting of pieces of wood, etc., to be used as lots. This is as likely as his own explanation, that " cut " is taken in the sense of " define," " decide."

Now with all deference to the scholarship of W. R. Smith and Wellhausen, I venture to think that they have not sufficiently considered the difference between *early* usage and *later*. It is almost certain that at first magic and divination were not discriminated : words used for one were used for the other. The fact that קֶסֶם has the sense of divination mostly, does not prove that its root and original meaning is this. I have already referred to an example of the use of magical means to obtain an oracle; in other words, among the Egyptians the priests divined by means of magic. (See page 28.)

That קָסַם denoted in the first place magical conjuration, note the use of the Arabic word قسم in its second and fourth forms, and the meaning of قَسَامَة an oath.

The Syriac أوֹמֵי to exorcise, the aphel form of ‏يَمَا or يِمَا to swear, is evidence of the same kind.

Then look at the Greek expression ὅρκια τέμνεσθαι, which occurs in Herodotus iv. 70, 71, 201, Homer Il. iv. 155, and in other Greek writers in the sense of making an oath with, then to make a covenant with. τέμνω has the same radical meaning as קסם, i.e. to cut, divide. I think in both cases there is an original reference to sacrifice, such as accompanied covenants as well as magical oaths. Cf. the phrases כָּרַת בְּרִית, icĕre (and ferire, percutere) foedus.

As regards actual usage, קסם means some form of divination in most cases. But it is so far from being certain that this is the primary meaning of the word, that the contrary view, advocated by Fleischer, is probably the right one.

The word acquired so wide a signification as to stand for divining by means of the ōb אוֹב (in 1 Samuel xxviii. 8).

With W. R. Smith and Wellhausen there can be no quarrel when they say that Qesem has originally a religious meaning. This is true of all the terms used for both magic and divination.

2. Consider next the root כשׁף. Several considerations unite in helping to understand the exact meaning of the word.

First, there is the etymology, which, however, is very uncertain. The old view is that we have the root in the

Arabic كَشَفَ, which means to uncover, to reveal. Divination would in that case be the primary sense. Against this is, however, the fact that Arabic ف corresponds to Hebrew שׁ or ס, not שׂ, and that כְּשָׁפִים in Micah v. 11, denotes material drugs, and is rendered by the LXX. φάρμακα.

Fleischer[1] argues for its derivation from كَسَفَ to eclipse, of sun, moon (God being subject). Then to be eclipsed, darkened. From this comes the meaning to look dark, troubled; to sink (of the eyes); become low (of the voice), so to speak in a low, murmuring tone. Then to pray. The Aramaic usage goes well with this, as أَكْشِف = to supplicate, entreat. But why not be content with the middle meaning, to be troubled, to look gloomy, distressed? This attitude well suits the suppliant.

We may have in כשׁף the same idea that lies in כסף, to be obscure, indistinct; then pale, white—the suppliant's face taking this colour. Dialectically, there is nothing in the way of this identification, as Arabic س = Hebrew ס (سمر = סמר, to nail) as well as שׂ (سمر = שׁמר, to wake by night). The מְכַשֵּׁף would then be a pale-faced, troubled one, cf. كاسف, unlucky, of days. The magician as wonder-worker, and also as diviner, frequently emaciating himself by fasting, sought special communion with the spirit world; cf. possible derivation of נחשׁ from حَسَّ, to be hungry.

Is it possible that in כשׁף = כסף, "to be white," we have a hint of the source of the later designation *White Magic*, שׂחר, in Isaiah xlvii. 11, if it is right to connect it with سحر, having in it the idea of *Black Magic*, שׁחר =

---

[1] Levy's "Neuheb. Wört.," ii. 459a.

black, cf. under שׁחר, p. 57 ff. W. R. Smith[1] traces כשׁף
to Arabic كسف in sense of " to cut," and he refers for
explanation to that feature of Semitic religion in which
worshippers cut themselves when appearing before deity.[2]

כְּשָׁפִים (a noun from the root of the verb) are, he
thinks, " herbs or drugs shredded into a magic brew "
(cf. كِسَف, pl. of كِسْفَة, bits of a thing). This derivation
ives the best explanation of the noun כְּשָׁפִים in Micah.
f Fleischer's etymology or the modified one suggested
be right, כְּשָׁפִים would then be those ingredients which
were used in approaching deity.

It is not, however, so certain as W. R. Smith makes
it, that the term denotes something material. It may
mean the mere performances of the מְכַשֵּׁף. " To cut off
כַּ from thine hands " can have a figurative sense as well
as a literal one.

The LXX. rendering is not strong enough even with the
help of מִיָּדִךְ to establish the material sense of כְּשָׁפִים.
In 2 Kings ix. 22, Nah. iii. 4, the LXX. renders the word
by φάρμακα, but in neither of these passages can it mean
drugs, nor can it have this meaning in Isa. xlii. 9, 12
(LXX. φαρμακεία) or in Num. xxiii. 3.[3]

Hebrew כשׁף is commonly represented in the Syriac
version by ܚܪܫܐ. מְכַשֵּׁף in Deut. xviii. 10 = ܚܪܫܐ,
כְּשָׁפִים = ܚܪܫܐ. In all the twelve instances in which
some form of כשׁף occurs in the Old Testament, it is

---

[1] Journ. Phil., xiv. p. 125.

[2] See 1 Kings xviii. 28 (re worshippers of Baal) and Jer. xli. 5.
(Men came from Shiloh and Samaria, with shaven beards and with
bodies that were cut, carrying offerings.)

[3] Where read with Kuenen וילך לכשפיו.

E

some form of ܡܙܚܒ that is made to translate it in the Peshiṭta.

What then does ܡܙܚܒ mean ? W. R. Smith, in order to find support for his view that כשף="to cut," suggests that ܡܙܚܒ is of the same origin as the Arabic خرس and خريسة, which mean the peculiar food given to women in childbed, and which was a drug, thus agreeing exactly with φάρμακα. But surely there is in the Syriac language itself an explanation of ܡܙܚܒ, for this very word means also to be silent, being equivalent to Hebrew חרש (especially Hi.) and Arabic خرس. The ܡܙܚܒܐ, following this etymology, is one that speaks in a low mumbling tone—one that restrains his speech.

Fried. Delitzsch [1] connects the root with the Assyrian Kharâshu, which has the meaning of restraining, compelling, binding.[2] This last supplies the best clue to the magical signification of ܡܙܚܒ, and it is the common idea out of which that of being silent, restraining one's self, etc., arises.

W. R. Smith's etymology, based as it is on a rare Arabic word, is far less likely than an etymology which is common to the principal Semitic languages.

3. The verb לָחַשׁ (lakhash), found in Aramaic and in Rabbinical Hebrew with the sense of "to hiss, as a serpent," is in my opinion a denominative from לָחַשׁ (lakhash), which is merely a dialectical variety of נָחַשׁ (nakhash), a serpent. ל and נ are both liquids, and both tend to fall out, as the nun in פ״ן verbs, and the ל in לָקַח.

Cf. also the imperfect of ܡܠܟ, imperf. ܢܡܠܟ, and the

---

[1] Proleg., p. 100.   [2] Cf. חבר and the magical tying.

occultation of ـلـ in أُوكِمِ. In the following words
לֹ and וֹ change places, with little, if any, difference of
meaning : לְשִׁכָּה and לחץ both signify to oppress ; לְשִׁכָּה
and נִשְׁכָּה both mean cell or chamber; צֶלֶם=صَنَم, image.
In the Arabic dialects نَقَم=لَقَم, while لقى and لقى inter-
change with each other. The form with לֹ is kept in the
O.T. mainly for the department of magic ; נָחַשׁ is used
almost wholly in connection with divination. Not at all
unlikely, the change came about through a desire, more
instinctive than conscious, to use different words for
different things.

Another tie uniting both words is the common meaning of unlucky, which is found in each of the Arabic
equivalents لحس (lahasa) (as لَحُوس lahus, unlucky, لَحِسَة
unfortunate year), and نَحَسَ (nahasa), نَحْس (nahs), unlucky, unhappy. This bad meaning which attaches to
both words arises probably through their connection
with the serpent, regarded as an evil spirit.

The objection which W. R. Smith urges against
making the verbs לָחַשׁ (lakhash) and נָחַשׁ (nakhash)
denominatives, that נָחַשׁ, in the sense of serpent, occurs
in no Semitic language except Hebrew, is not conclusive,
for in each of these languages there are words derived
from simpler forms found only in some one sister tongue.
Nor does Smith adhere to the principle laid down in this
connection, since he explains מְעוֹנֵן (me'onen) from
غَنّ (ghanna), a word which occurs only in Arabic, just
as he connects Syriac ܚܪܫ (kheresh) with the root
خَرَس or خَرِسَة found in Arabic alone, and but rarely in this
language. The place held by the serpent in ancient

religions must be here assumed. On the matter the following works may be consulted, "The Worship of the
Serpent," by Rev. J. Deane, London, 1832, 2nd edition,
1833, considerably enlarged; "Tree and Serpent Worship," by James Fergusson, 1868 and 1873; Baudissen's
"Studien zur Semit. Religions-geschichte," i. 256 ff.;
"Götzendienst u. Zauberwesen," etc., Scholz, p. 79 f.;
Wellhausen's "Reste," p. 152 f. One of the earliest
Gnostic sects, if not the earliest, goes by the name
of Ophites (ὄφις) and Na'asites (נָחָשׁ), because the symbol
of the serpent was central in their ritual and theology.
Cf. שָׂרָף (serpent), in Isa. xiv. 29, xxx. 6. Wellhausen
thinks there is reference in these passages to the place
of the serpent in the old religions.[1]

In Eccles. x. 11, and in Jer. viii. 17 לַחַשׁ (lakhash)
stands for a snake charm, something which prevents the
snake from biting. In both verses לַחַשׁ (lakhash) and נָחָשׁ
(nakhash) are brought together as happy and designed
antitheses, though both originally sprang from the same
root. Since the serpent represented an evil spirit, and even
the devil,[2] לַחַשׁ (lakhash) came to mean a charm against
any demon, and the מְלַחֵשׁ (melakhesh) a charmer against
any and every evil spirit, as in Isa. ii. 3.

The ornaments mentioned in Isa. iii. 20 were originally
amulets to protect against demons. Among them
לְחָשִׁים (lekhashim) are named. What exact shape these
were of, is a matter of uncertainty; but as the next
words stand for finger-rings and nose-rings, it is not at
all unlikely that this word stands for ear-rings, which

---

[1] See Wellh. Reste, p. 155.
[2] See Smend, p. 119; cf. the serpent that tempted Eve; see also
Grimm, p. 998.

were certainly amulets, as is shown by Gen. xxxv. 4
(בָּאָזְנֵיהֶם אֲשֶׁר נְזָמִים=Targ. קָדָשַׁיָּא=Syr. مَهَا).[1]

The two latter words are used in Isa. iii. 20 for לְחָשִׁים.
Dr. Smith so explains לַחַשׁ, and he is probably right. In
Isa. xxvi. 16 לַחַשׁ denotes prayer, a meaning easily
deducible from incantation. But the text of this verse
appears to be corrupt.

לחשׁ is so closely connected with demonology that it
might have been left to that part of this treatise. But
it belongs also to magic, as all amulets necessarily do, and
it seemed advisable to deal with this species of magic
before the next is dealt with, as both are closely connected by W. R. S.[2]

4. חֶבֶר (kheber), חֹבֵר (khober). There are but three
places in the Old Testament in which חבר, as noun or as
verb, has a significance for magic. These are Deut.
xviii. 11 (חֹבֵר חָבֶר), Ps. lviii. 6 (הֹבֵר חֲבָרִים), and Isa.
xlvii. 9, 12, twice (חֲבָרִים).

In Ps. lviii. 6 קוֹל מְלַחֲשִׁים is followed immediately by
חֹבֵר חֲבָרִים. W. R. Smith concludes that the same
thing is meant by both, the parallelism, he thinks,
showing this. The conception at the root of חבר is, he
alleges, snake-charming. חֶבֶר is therefore like לַחַשׁ,
a charm against the snake. This view is at least as old
as the Talmud[3]; it is defended by Pseudo-Jonathan, and
by Rashi (see his commentary on Deut. xviii. 10).
In the Talmud, however, a distinction is made between

---

[1] Perhaps by לחשׁ we are to understand a serpent-shaped ear-ring,
so formed because designed, on the principle of symbolic magic, to be a
countercharm against the snake. Cf. p. 38 ff.

[2] Journ. Phil., xiv. p. 114 f.   [3] See Jebam, 121a.

the great Khober חֶבֶר גָּדוֹל, who exercises his magic upon great animals, and the small Khober חֶבֶר קָטֹן, who uses it against smaller animals—serpents, scorpions, insects, etc. (See Brecher, p. 138.) Smith would have done better to follow Gesenius (Thes. i. 441), who interprets חבר literally to bind, of magical knots, than to go back to the baseless Jewish traditional explanation. It shows the enormous influence of this great English scholar that Buhl (Ges.[12]) and Sigfried and Stade in their lexicons, Stade in his Geschichte (i. 105), and Driver in his commentary on Deut. xviii. 10, tread in his steps; yet the evidence is of the slightest. The word חבר refers to the *effect*, not to the *cause* or instrumentality.

Incantations as well as amulets were used to bind demons. To these the deaf adder stops his ears, Ps. lviii. 5. He listens not to the sound of the magician, bind they ever so cleverly.

Parallelism, on which Rob. Smith bases his argument, does not mean that words thus joined have identical meanings. We need not travel beyond the Psalm referred to in order to show this. In ver. 4 רְשָׁעִים is parallel with דֹּבְרֵי כָזָב, and זֹרוּ with תָּעוּ. Who would infer that therefore the words thus related have the same shade of meaning?

Moreover, in the other passages, Deut. xviii. 11, Isa. xlvii. 9, 12, חֲבָרִים is parallel to כְּשָׁפִים, and it is the more striking that in the same chapter of Isaiah, both these words are found together in v. 9 and in v. 12. If parallelism is to decide, it is most certainly in favour of making חֲבָרִים and כְּשָׁפִים identical in meaning, rather than לְחַשִׁים and חֲבָרִים.

חָבַר means "to tie, bind," in Hebrew, Aramaic and Ethiopic, and gets its sense in magic from the fact that the person using חָבַר binds the spirits or gods. It is in the same sense that the Greeks used καταδέω (see references in Passow, "Handwörterbuch der Griechischen Sprache," 5te Auflage, vol. i. p. 160a), the Romans "ligare, ligulam," the Arabs عقد السحر, مربط, the Germans "Nestel knüpfen," and the English "magic knots." In all this we have traces of what we call sympathetic, or, what Tylor calls, symbolic magic.

R. Smith thinks the binding refers to the words: words *bound*, so as to constitute a magical formula. Gesenius suggests this too, though at the expense of consistency. (See *loc. cit.*) The binding in that case refers to the *words*, not the magical *act* implied. Upon the face of it, this is unlikely, as the analogy of Aramaic, Ethiopic, as well as that of modern languages shows.

Dr. Smith supports his view that חָבַר חֶבֶר = nectere verba, from the Arabic خبر "a narrative, that which is fastened together." Now, the root meaning of خبر is "to know"; in the 4th form, أخبر "to make to know." خبر is a communication of knowledge. In no instance does the word convey the notion of binding. Far more likely is the connection of חבר with the Arabic حبر. Hebrew ח = Arabic خ (as חָרַשׁ = خرس "to be deaf and dumb") and ح (as חָרַשׁ "to cut, plough" = حرث). The connection of Hebrew (and Syriac) חבר with حبر is thus linguistically possible. Some additional considerations render it probable. According to Lane (*sub voce*) حبر means "to make beautiful" (of handwriting, poetry, language, science, etc.). Freytag also gives *pulchrum fecit*

as the fundamental meaning. Now, this would most
naturally arise out of an earlier meaning of "to bind";
thus, to fasten together words so as to make beautiful
sentences, thoughts, and the like. Moreover, both
Freytag and Lane explain خَبَر as a sweet, a beautiful
melody, which connects خبر with magical intonation.
Again, חָבֵר in Hebrew means a companion, an associate;
in later Hebrew, a member of the same society, guild;
then, a Jewish priest or doctor. This word is represented
in N Arabic by خَبَر and خِبَر; cf. خَبَرانِيَّة "pontifical"
in modern Arabic. These last may be, however, mere
loan words; but even the representation of Hebrew ח by
Arabic ح is significant for my argument. We have probably the same root in חָבַל "to bind," in the Arabic حَبَل
"to tie, bind," and حَبْل "a cord or halter to tie with."
Now the liquids (ל, מ, נ, ר) exchange freely in the Semitic
languages. (See Wright's "Comparative Grammar of
the Semitic Languages," Cambridge, 1890, p. 67 ff.)
Hebrew אַלְמָנָה ("widow") is in Syriac ܐܪܡܠܬܐ, and in
Arabic أَرْمَلَة. Thus, חבר, محبر, حبر, and حبل are all
dialectic variants of one common and original root
meaning "to bind"; while خبر seems to stand outside
of this category.

Before passing away from this *binding* magic, it is of
interest to note the Rabbinical word for "amulet,"
קָמִיַע, which comes from קמע (= قمع) "to bind, to master."
Its passive form makes it likely, however, that the קָמִיַע
is that which is *bound to the person*, as an amulet, and not
that which binds the Deity. This Hebrew word is used
for the Tephellin (Phylacteries), etc. (See Levy, Neu-
Heb. Wörterbuch, *sub voce*.)

It is not impossible that Christ's words to the disciples, "What things soever ye shall *bind* on earth shall be *bound* in heaven : and what things ye shall loose on earth shall be loosed in heaven" (Matt. xviii. 18), were suggested by this magical practice, known in His time and in His country as in all times and lands.

5. שַׁחַר (shakhar), in Isa. xlvii. 11, has since the time of J. H. Michaelis († 1738) been explained as referring to magic. (See his Annot. ad Biblia, 1720.) He was followed by J. D. Michaelis (Suppl. ad Lex. Heb., p. 2314), Koppe, Doed., Eichhorn, Hitzig, Ewald, De Wette, Dillmann (who reads שַׁחֲרָה), Kautzsch ("Heilige Schrift 'weg zu Zaubern ' "), Wellhausen ("Reste," p. 159, note 1, and "Israel. u. Jud. Gesch.," 1895, p. 100). So also margin of R.V.

The favour of this exegesis are the following considerations :—(1) It makes excellent sense. In the first clause the evil that will come is such as cannot be kept off by any magical incantation or amulet or drug, such as were used to keep off injuries due to demons ; in the second the destruction is such as no payment can prevent—it is beyond being expiated for. To be *charmed away* makes a good parallel with to *be bought* off, to be kept away by payment.

(2) The word employed here has its equivalent in the Arabic سحر, the word most commonly used for magic. The primary meaning of the verb سحر is to turn or transform a thing into something else, love into hatred, etc. The evil in this passage might well be described as that which could not be turned into anything else; it was, as such, inevitable.

(3) The words were written in Babylon where magic

was extensively cultivated. Assuming the root existing
in Arabic to be so old, the intelligent Babylonian native
or resident would be likely to be acquainted with it, as
the thing for which it stood was so rife around him.

(4) In the next verse two undoubted magical terms
are found, viz. חֲבָרִים (khebarim) and כְּשָׁפִים (keshaphim),
which shows that the idea of magic was in the writer's
mind. Yet, if the word has in this verse the sense first
claimed for it by J. H. Michaelis, it is strange that in the
whole range of Hebrew literature, ancient and modern,
it never again occurs with this meaning ; nor does
Aramaic (Syriac, or so-called Chaldee) supply one
solitary example of this signification.

Of the ancient versions the LXX. renders the verse
somewhat freely, but it represents שַׁחֲרָהּ (shakhrah) by
βάθυνος (=βόθρος), evidently reading שַׁחַת (shakhat).
In the Syriac we have ܒܨܦܪܐ, "in the morning," reading
בַּשַּׁחַר (bashshakhar). Not one of these gives a good
sense. Not the LXX., for the pit cannot be said to come
upon one ; not the Syriac, because "in the morning"
does not correspond to anything following it ; in fact,
the rest of the verse is very confused in this version.

In Ges.-Buhl's lexicon there is a happy suggestion,
though it has no support in the versions, nor before 1895
was it ever, I think, put forward, unless Sigfried and
Stade's lexicon hints at it. The first-named lexicon
would substitute שִׁחֲדָהּ (shikhadah), but as the Qal of
this verb is alone used, it would be better to read שְׁחָדָהּ
(shekhadah). The English will then be : " There shall
come upon thee an evil which thou art not able to
prevent by payment, and destruction shall fall upon thee

such as thou art not able to expiate." The verb is found in Job vi. 22 in the sense of paying a ransom to keep away some calamity.

In Prov. vi. 35 the nouns כֹּפֶר (kopher) and שֹׁחַד (shakhad) occur in corresponding members of the verse, just as the verbs do in Isaiah. The Proverbs passage may be thus put into English: "He will not be propitiated by any ransom; nor will he be well disposed though thou multiply thy gifts to him." Cheyne[1] adopts this emendation.

Magic in the New Testament.

I want to make one or two references to New Testament passages which also have to do more or less with magic among the Hebrews.

What has been called *Battologia* is derived from Battus (Βάττος), a Greek poet who used many repetitions or, according to Herodotus,[2] who stuttered. The word is, however, possibly mimetic. Whatever may be its etymology, the verb βαττολογέω has in Greek literature the meaning of prattling, babbling, excessive talking. (See the Greek lexicons.)

Among the ancients, repetitions of certain formulæ were considered efficacious in proportion to the number of repetitions. In India to-day, if an ascetic says in one month the name of Radha, Krishna or Ram 100,000 times, he cannot fail to obtain what he wants.

It is in the same spirit that Moslem dervishes renew their shrieks or whirlings: the more this is done the greater the power which Allah has over them.

[1] Sacred Books of the Old Test. "Isaiah": Addenda to Hebrew text.
[2] i. 155.

The prophets of Baal called upon their god from morning until night in the same spirit (1 Kings xviii. 25, saying, " Baal, hear us").

Christ, in the sermon on the mount, warns His hearers against believing that the efficacy of a prayer depends on the number of times it is said (Matt. vi. 7).

The words μὴ βαττολογήσητε[1] mean "Do not repeat yourselves" (in prayer), and have reference to the same superstition. Unless such a practice was in vogue among the Jews of His time, He would not have deemed it necessary to give this warning.

"Pray without ceasing" (1 Thess. v. 12) may have been suggested to the Apostle's mind by the superstitious habit of reiteration in prayer. "Keep on praying," i.e. "be always in the praying temper."

In Eisenmenger's "Endectes Judenthum," vol. i. 580 f., we read that when in the various synagogues prayer is separately said, these prayers are woven by an angel into a crown, which is set on God's head. The more the prayers, the larger the crown.

In 2 Tim. iii. 13, γόητες (from γοάω to sigh, utter low mournful tones) is used of a class of magicians who uttered certain prescribed magical formulæ in a low, deep voice. Herodotus described them as being in Egypt[2] and elsewhere ;[3] they are also mentioned by Euripides and Plato. The word is rendered by Luther "verführerische Menschen," and in the English versions by "impostor."

The Syriac Pesh. version gives ܡܛܥܝܢܐ "those who lead astray." The Hebrew New Testaments of Salkinson and of Delitzsch more correctly translate by מְקַסְּמִים for

---

[1] Cf. Eccles. viii. 14 : μὴ δευτερώσῃς λόγον ἐν προσευχῇ σου, " Do not repeat thy words in thy prayer." For references to Battology among Moslems and others, see Lange in Herzog, xviii. 396.

[2] ii. 33.

[3] iv. 105 ; vii. 191.

which, in English, " diviners " is mostly used. " Sorcerers " would be as near the original as any other English word.

Accepting W. Robertson Smith's etymology of מְעוֹנֵן, this word has a very similar meaning to γόητες; cf. Fleischer's derivation of כָּשַׁף from كَسَفَ, to speak in a low murmuring tone.[1]

Paul, in addressing the Galatians, names among the works of the flesh φαρμακεία (Eng. VV. "sorcery"; Syr. ܟ݂ܰܪܳܫܽܘܬ݂ܳܐ kharashuta.; Hebrew Testaments of Salk. and Del. כְּשָׁפִים keshaphim), which is closely connected with " idolatry " by being put next after it (Gal. v. 20).

It is not possible here to do more than mention Simon Magus, or Simon the Magician (Acts viii. 9 f.), and Bar-jesus the Sorcerer, whom Luke calls also Elymas (Acts xiii. 8). This latter name the writer explains by ὁ μάγος; it is really the Arabic عَلِيم 'aleem (or عَالِم 'ālim), "learned," which is much the same in sense as μάγος.

Post-Biblical Judaism.

As later Jewish magic is for the most part associated with belief in the existence and power of demons, much on this subject will be found under the head of " Demonology."

In the main Dr. Rabbi D. Joel[2] is right in claiming for the Mishna comparative freedom from magical principles. That is due largely to the fact that in the Mishna we have a collection of the laws and principles which were to guide the Jew : the Oral law (תּוֹרָה שֶׁבְּעַל פֶּה) as opposed to the written (תּוֹרָה שֶׁבִּכְתָב).

Nevertheless, if the belief in magic were common among

See *supra*, p. 48.   [2] Der Aber. p. 34 .

the Jews of the first and second centuries of our era, and if it were approved by the national leaders, we should expect to find regulations concerning it in this law book. But we look in vain for anything of the kind.

In the Talmud, however, there are many acknowledgments of the existence among the Jews in Palestine and Babylon of magical superstitions. Joel quotes examples, though he is too anxious to make little of them, and to claim for his co-religionists a freedom from superstition which they have no right to claim. Where the later Jews got their magic from is a debated and debatable question. See a discussion of this question at page 114 ff. I will anticipate so much as to say that there is a growing tendency to make Gnosticism the principal source of later Jewish magic and demonology. This Gnosticism is for the most part a growth out of the native Babylonian religion, but in it we have a remarkable syncretism of elements, belonging in the main to Babylon, but also to Greece (Neoplatonism), Egypt and Persia. In Gnosticism, as in Judaism, names and numbers play a great *rôle*.

In many of the old religions, names of deities were credited with extraordinary power. He who used them was master of the god. As the priests grew in power, they claimed the exclusive knowledge of these names. We have an instance of this in the Tetragrammaton.[1] It has been the custom to trace the sacredness of this name to the Pythagorean Tetraktys, or mystic number of four. Dr. Gaster sees in the Gnostic "Tetraktys"— formed by combining the first two divine sysygies or

---

[1] The four consonants of the Hebrew word for Yahwe. The vowel-sounds were included in what we now call consonants, as in Assyrian, Ethiopic, and originally in all Semitic languages.

pairs—the real counterpart of the Hebrew "Four-letter-word."

But, whatever the source, there is no denying the fact of the sacred and all-prevailing efficacy of "Yahve." He who, in his prayer, was able to use this name, was sure to get what he asked for. Prayer was often fruitless just because this name was left out. (Eisenmenger i. 581 f.) Compare with this the place given in the New Testament to *name* as standing for the person (John i. 12). When other names got to be substituted for the *Tetragrammaton*, they in their turn were believed to have the same mystic power. Belief in angels grew, and it was soon thought that *their* names, when used in certain formulæ, had an influence, less indeed, but not less real than those of Yahve. Names of God and of angels were varied in ways familiar to students of the Qabbalah.[1] So in many old Jewish incantations the most bewildering names present themselves. The most complete and important monument of mediæval Jewish magic is the "Sword of Moses," the original text of which has been recently found by Dr. Gaster. He gives a complete translation in *Asiatic Journal*, January, 1896, p. 175 ff., together with an account of the discovery and character of the MS. A reference to this will show the most extraordinary combinations of letters to form names which exists in any language.

MAGIC AMONG ARABS AND MOSLEMS.

In tracing the history of religious thought and custom among the Arabs, we have the disadvantage that the literature of this people is comparatively recent ; none

---

[1] See Ginsburg's Kabb., p. 49 f.

of it going further back than, say, a century or two before the appearance of Mohammed. Of pre-Islamic literature, not only have we but little preserved, but that little is nearly altogether poetry (Mo‘allaqât, etc.). Freytag, in his Einleitung, etc., and Wellhausen, in his "Reste," etc., have gathered together in their valuable books such notices as they have found in Arabic literature, bearing upon the subjects under consideration. Freytag's work is not nearly as well known as it ought to be, though it is lacking in that conciseness and accuracy by which Wellhausen's book is marked. As regards magic, both these writers concern themselves mainly with its demonological side : Wellhausen deals at length with what he calls "Gegenzauber" (counptercharm), which he defines as the "art of making demons harmless and of scaring them away."

This is the principal use to which, among the primitive Arabs, magic was put. I shall return to this when dealing with demonology.

Mohammed, from the standpoint of monotheism, stoutly opposed that kind of magic for which سِحْر stands, as it was associated with heathenism and involved appeals to other spiritual beings than God. For the same reason he condemned divination, as it is represented by the word كَهَانَة. On the other hand, among orthodox Moslems, almost if not quite from the Prophet's day, the system of magic covered by دَعْوَة has been regarded as permissive, because in it only God and good angels are invoked. It is probable, indeed, that the Prophet did not allow any but Allah to be thus recognized, as is the case among those Moslem Puritans, the Wahhabees, at the present day.

There is a very elaborate science giving details as to how the incantations called دَعْوَات are to be recited and the results interpreted. The best native work on the subject is the " Juwahiree 'l-Khamsat," by Sheikh Abu 'l-Muwayyid of Gergerat, A.H. 956. Hughes, in his Dictionary of Islam, gives an epitome of as much of the work as is not peculiar to Indian Islam.[1]

The word دَعْوَة in its magical sense does not occur in the Quran, though in its ordinary meaning of prayer it is found six times.

The spell or charm termed Ruqya (رُقْيَة) was also allowed by the Prophet, so says Anas, whose words are given by Hughes.[2]

Ruqya was made up of passages from the Quran, either spoken, or written on an amulet which was worn, the purpose being to keep off the evil eye, epilepsy, etc., which were believed to be the work of demons.[3]

The Quran has the word four times, or, if we include the doubtful case الترقى, five times. In all but one it has its usual meaning "to ascend." In Sura lxxv. 27 راق appears to denote "magician." There is no opinion expressed as to whether or not the راق is approved of. Perhaps the word does not in this case depart from its connotation in the other places, the question then being, "Who is able to arise out of the calamity newly described ?"

عَزِيمَة is another magical term in use among the Arabs. The word denotes strictly " determination," from عزم " to resolve," and is not found in this form or (magical) sense in the Quran. It denotes a charm consisting of Quran

---

[1] See p. 72 ff.　　[2] Ib., p. 303b.　　[3] See DEMONOLOGY.

verses recited with the intention of removing sickness. Arabic writers distinguish between عَزَائِمُ ٱلْقُرْآن, which aim at influencing Allah, and هـ ٱلرّقَى, which have the purpose of immediately acting against the Jinns or demons.[1]

عُوذَة from عَاذَ (عوذ) stands for an amulet worn upon the person, as phylacteries by the Jews, to protect against demons, but especially against the evil eye.[2] Probably it had on it the 113th or 114th suras of the Quran, perhaps both. It is for this reason that these suras get the name مُعَوِّذَتَان, though some will have it that this name is given to them because each begins with قُلْ أَعُوذُ.

It is interesting to note that in Sura 113 we read of the magic knot عُقَد plural of عُقْدَة. مَعَاذَة and تَعْوِيذ are used interchangeably with عُوذَة.

The next word to note in this connection is تَمِيمَة, which has been wrongly identified with عُوذَة. This last consists, as has been seen, of an amulet with a Quran inscription. تَمِيمَة, on the other hand, is a black bead speckled with white, though there is room for doubt as to its exact shape.

Freytag, however, followed by Wellhausen,[3] says it is a necklace and not a bead, as Lane maintains. Besides differing in form from عُوذَة its use was forbidden by Mohammed, while the former was allowed. A connection is suggested by Freytag with the תֻּמִּים worn by the high priest, Deut. xxxiii. 8, etc. Later Jewish scholars think that this has some connection with magic.

Gildemeister considers تَمِيمَة to be a mere transcription of the Greek Telesma (τέλεσμα), whence the English

---

[1] See Wellh. Reste, 161, note 3.   [2] Ib., p. 165, note 4.
[3] Wellh. Reste, p. 166.

"talisman." The usual explanation of the word is that it comes from تَمَّ (to be complete), because it was believed to keep the person whole or healthy.

The tamima was worn by women and children only. As the boy grew up to manhood this amulet was taken from his neck. Though Islam disowns the name, this kind of amulet is still to be seen worn by the Meccan boys.

حِجاب (strictly what hinders, keeps off) is used to describe an amulet which was kept in a case called بَيْت حِجاب and suspended on the right side by a string passing over the left shoulder, or on some other part of the person.

These words belong more to DEMONOLOGY than to magic in its narrow sense, but it seemed desirable to give in one place a short account of the Arabic terms.

ASSYRIAN MAGIC.

It is impossible here to supply more than a brief summary of results to which we are led by the able works of Lenormant, Tallqvist, Zimmern, King, mentioned in my list of authorities.

What Lenormant maintains in his "Chaldean Magic"—that the magic of the Babylonians and Assyrians was handed on to them by the Accadians—is now generally admitted.

But it was reserved for their successors to systematize the magic which they received from the Accadians, and to have it regulated and protected by the state.

Among the Babylonians and Assyrians there were two kinds of magicians.

ILLEGAL MAGIC.

I. There were those wizards and witches belonging to the olden time, who practised their art in simple ways, having no elaborate ritual or written incantations. They were supposed to have to do with demons, and to be in league with them in bringing bad dreams, misfortune, diseases, death, etc., upon people. They were therefore condemned by the government and subjected to severe penalties for carrying on their trade. Among those who practised this magic were both men and women.

The names by which the men are known in the Cuneiform inscriptions are kašapu (=מְכַשֵּׁף), epišu, saḫiru, raḫû. The women were known by corresponding names with the feminine ending, kašaptu, epištu, saḫirtu, raḫirtu, etc.

Singular to say, the females, whom we may call witches—reserving "wizards" for the male, were greatly in the ascendency, and seemed to do nearly all the work.

In the Old Testament the existence of witches is implied in Ex. xxii. 17, "Thou shalt not suffer a sorceress (מְכַשֵּׁפָה) to live"; and in the account of the Witch of Endor (בַּעֲלַת אוֹב) in 1 Sam. xxviii. 3 ff.

Wizards and witches were credited with the ability to tear people's hair and clothes, to bring about sickness and even death. They could cause delusions and insanity. Families were divided by discord, lovers were made to hate each other.

Not only had they power over human beings, but they could bring into subjection to them the demons themselves.

The means they employed were the evil eye, evil

ongue and the evil mouth. But it was the evil word
or imprecation that was most powerful.

They tied magic knots, and other acts are assigned to
them which we do not clearly understand. Their best
known contrivance was to make an image of the person
to be acted upon, and to treat this—cut, burn, etc.—just
as they wanted the person whose image it was to be
dealt with. This is really what we now call " sympathetic
magic," and it is interesting to note how ancient and
widespread this was.

Legal Magic.

Now we come to the class of recognized magicians who
were called Eššepu or Aššipu, the same word as the
Hebrew אַשָּׁף and the Syriac ܐܫܘܦܐ.

These were the official magicians, and received from
the state recognition and support. As opposed to the
wizards and witches, their immediate intercourse was
with the good spirits, especially with Ea, her sons Šamaš,
Marduk, Gibil, and Misku, together with her daughter
Ishtar and her husband Tammuz.

The contrast between the two classes is to be compared
with the more modern distinction of black and white
magic.

In regard to black magic it will be noted that among
the Babylonians, as well as among more modern nations,
woman is a more prominent figure than man. So in
Eden she was first in disobedience.

Mark too that, though among the Babylonians the
good spirits were sought to by the official magicians, yet
the purpose was mainly to obtain protection from the
evil spirits. Worship, prayer, as we find them among

the Hebrews, was rare yet not absent. The interesting collection of prayers published and translated in Mr. King's "Bab. Magic" shows that the Babylonians could offer prayers, as earnest and even as spiritual as the Hebrews. Nevertheless the principal means employed were forms of incantation, medicaments, etc.

But the Babylonian Eššepu was more than anything else an exorcist, and this section might, with as much appropriateness, have found its place under DEMONOLOGY.

Like the wizards and witches, the exorcists (Aššipi) made much use of the image, and in a similar way. Sometimes one material was used to make the likeness of the person ; sometimes different ingredients were used for the different parts of the body. But the instruments of their art were chiefly medicines, drinks, foods, ointments, ablution and purification. These were certainly in some cases adapted to secure the end desired, and they were selected for this reason. Indeed, in the later and more developed magic of the Babylonians, we have the beginnings of medical science, just as in their astrology we have the beginnings of astronomy. There is some honest striving after the truth in the most lame and grotesque attempts that infant man has made to discover the secrets of the world ; and he has never quite missed the mark.

EGYPTIAN MAGIC.

There were two sides to MAGIC in Egypt as in Assyria. It could be used for the benefit of the human race or to the detriment of the same.

Each man's fate was fixed, and what that was could be found out from the planet under which the individual was born. Yet these fates could be controlled by the gods, who often interfered for the purpose of saving their favourites. Even man had power by specific acts and agents to overrule the fixtures of fate. The dead could be overmastered and indeed the gods themselves.

The medical science of the Egyptians was closely connected with their magic, or rather demonology.

The human body was divided into thirty-six parts, and over each of these a deity presided. To keep on good terms with the respective deity was to preserve the part well. This is brought out in chapter xlii. of the "Book of the Dead," from which it appears that Nu saw to the hair, Ra to the face, Hather to the eyes, Assûat to the ears, Anubis to the lips, while Theth had charge of the body in general.

Disease was considered due to demons, and certain formulæ were recited, sometimes to be said over and over before they could be successful. The patient swallowed formulæ written on papyrus; amulets were worn.

For further details, see Wied. p. 261 to end.

II. DIVINATION.

DEFINITION.

DIVINATION is the art of obtaining special information from spiritual beings.

Dr. E. B. Tylor[1] and Dr. F. B. Jevons[2] make a distinction between divination due to supernatural agency and such as is not, but may be called natural. All divination, however, conforms to the definition given above. If the changes through which the lock of a person's hair passes indicate the varying conditions of the person whose lock it is, this is due to the belief actual or implied that some superior power deigns to make the former phenomena significant of the latter. Or if, to adduce Tylor's instance, a tree planted at the birth of a child is held by its flourishing or otherwise to reveal the course of the child's life, it is because some superior intelligence is pleased by the vicissitudes of the tree to tell the tale of the human life. "Omens," says W. Robertson Smith, "are not blind tokens; the animals know what they tell to man."[3]

[1] "Encyc. Brit.," 9 ("Divination").
[2] Clark's "Bible Dictionary" ("Divination").
[3] "Religion of the Semites," p. 424.

Divination and Biblical Prophecy.

It is exceedingly difficult, if indeed possible, to indicate the boundary line between divination and prophecy. In both the same general principle obtains—intercourse on the part of man with the spiritual world in order to obtain special knowledge. In divination this knowledge is usually got by observing certain omens or signs ; but this is by no means always the case, since sometimes the beings consulted "possessed" the soothsayer, just as spiritualistic mediums claim to be "possessed." The diviner and the modern "medium" profess alike to be channels through which spiritual beings speak.[1] Divination, as practised in this last method, does not differ from Biblical prophecy of the lowest kind—that of the ecstatic state, as distinguished from the higher species of prophecy which, in Riehm's happy phrase, is "psychologically mediated."[2]

The word "prophecy" is mostly employed of communications from God in the Old and New Testament sense. Of necessity, therefore, it stands upon higher ground than divination in the usual heathen sense of the word. But the ordinary theological distinction is unjust and opposed to Semitic etymology.[3] When the Israelites resorted to magic and divination,[4] it was in the belief that Yahwe sanctioned and controlled these practices and accepted them as legitimate. The diviner among Arabs, Greeks, and Romans was often as sincere as Isaiah or Jeremiah, and who will deny that to him, as

---

[1] See Dr. Granger's "Worship of the Romans," p. 174.
[2] "Messianic Prophecy," p. 45 *et passim*.
[3] See Hofmann's "Weissagung und Erfüllung," i. p. 12.
[4] Cf. Deut. xviii. 10, 11.

well as to the Old Testament seer, God spake in very truth?[1] Belief in the special mission and authority of the Israelitish prophet does not carry with it the implication that the diviners or prophets of other nations and of other religions were impostors. W. Robertson Smith[2] and others[3] have shown that the religion of the Old Testament has many elements which are common to other Semitic religions, and even to non-Semitic religions.

METHODS.

There were among the ancient Greeks, Romans, Arabs, etc., modes of divining which were apparently unknown to the Hebrews of the Old Testament : e.g. by observation of the flights and cries of birds, inspection of the entrails of animals, etc. Dr. Granger's " Worship of the Romans," p. 173 ff. (Freytag, " Einleitung," p. 159 ff.)

Yet there are many signs or omens mentioned in the Old Testament which are either similar to or identical with those made use of among other nations.

1. Belomancy was practised among the Arabs,[4] and also among the Chaldeans.[5] The Israelites were also sometimes addicted to this ; the monotheistic prophets indeed forbade it, but it probably existed uncondemned in earlier times. The " wood " and " staff " in Hosea iv. 12, stand for the same thing, the first denoting the material, and the second the form into

[1] See Briggs' " Messianic Prophecy," p. 4 f. Cf. *per contra*, Orelli, " Old Testament Prophecy," p. 24.
[2] " Religion of the Semites."
[3] See Cobb's " Origenes Judaicæ " ; Schultz's " Old Testamen Theology," i. p. 250 ff.
[4] Wellhausen, " Reste," 132.
[5] Lenormant, " La Divination," chs. ii. and iv. Sayce, " T. S. Bibl. Arch.," iii. 145.

which it was made. There is no doubt that we are to understand the same kind of divination as that 'practised by the Babylonian king.[1]

2. The Babylonian king is represented in the Ezekiel passage just quoted as looking at the liver, that is the liver of an animal offered in sacrifice, with a view to divination. Animals were often sacrificed in order to propitiate the god or gods consulted, so that the special intimations sought might be granted. We have an example of this in the history of Balaam, Num. xxiii. 1, 2, 14.[2]

3. " Sortilege " or divination by lot was a very common method of divining among the Arabs[3] and Romans[4] The " Urim and Thummim " were simply two stones put into the pocket attached to the high priest's ephod ; on them were written some such words as " yes " and " no." Whichever stone was taken out, the alternative word upon it was looked upon as the divine decision. Probably whenever we have the phrase שָׁאַל בְּ (" to inquire of," see 1 Sam. xiv. 37, xxiii. 2, etc.), we are to understand the appeal to the priest made by " Urim and Thummim." Cf. Jonah i. 7 ff., where we read that the mariners cast lots to find out on account of whom the storm was. No condemnation is expressed in the Biblical narrative.

4. We have other signs recognized in the Old Testament, as in Judges vi. 36 (Gideon's fleece), and in 1 Sam. xiv. 8 ff. (Jonathan decides whether or not he is to

---

[1] See Ezek. xxi. 23 ff., where we read of arrows being used. Cf. the two Greek words βελομαντεία and ῥαβδομαντεία.
[2] Well. " Reste," p. 133.
[3] Well. " Reste," ii. 134 f.
[4] Smith, " Dict. of Antiq.," art. " Sortes."

attack the Philistines by the words which he may happen to hear them speak).

5. Of astrological beliefs and practices the early Israelites seem to have been quite ignorant. In the Old Testament there is no passage older than the Exile that shows acquaintance with such beliefs and practices. Deutero-Isaiah (xlvii. 13) has these words : "Thou art wearied in the multitude of thy counsels ; let now the astrologers,[1] the stargazers, the monthly prognosticators, stand up and save thee from the things that shall come upon thee."

In Jeremiah x. 3 the people are warned against the way of the heathen, lest they be terrified by signs in the sky, as were the Assyrians and Babylonians. The prophet's words are these : "Thus saith Yahwe, learn not the way of the nations and be not dismayed at the signs of heaven : for the nations are dismayed at them." The whole section (x. 1—16) of which this forms a part, is probably the work of the Redactor of Jeremiah (so Cheyne, Pulpit Commentary), and was addressed to Israel in Babylon, warning them against the idolatrous practices carried on around them.

These two Exilic passages support the belief that it was during the residence in Babylon that the Hebrews came for the first time into contact with astrological usages. When we come to the Book of Daniel astrology is countenanced. The Book was written in the first half of the second century B.C., and reflects the prevailing thought of the Palestinian Jews at the time of its composition. Daniel—the ideal Jew—is made head of the wise

---

[1] הֹבְרֵי שָׁמַיִם, "dividers of the heavens;" LXX. ἀστρολόγοι τοῦ οὐρανοῦ.

men[1] in Babylon (ii. 48), i.e. of all the diviners, whether or not they divine by stars. In iv. 6 we are told that he was made chief of the "learned ones"[2] (khartummayya), a term which, like "wise men," includes all the diviners and magicians.[3] That astrologers are embraced appears from v. 11, where this generic term stands first, the other words following by way of explanation.

Note also the approval with which, in Matt. ii., the conduct of the wise men, who were guided by celestial omens, is regarded.

6. The most important of all the modes of divination which link the Hebrews with other nations is that by dreams. In fact, dream divination among the Hebrews differs hardly if at all from that which obtained among the Greeks and other nations of antiquity. It is supposed that the dream is introduced from outwards into the human soul in order to convey some intimation. Jacob may have sufficient reason for making good his escape from Laban, but he will not take the decisive step without a direct revelation, which revelation comes to him in a dream (Gen. xxxi. 10—13). His resolution becomes objective as a dream. In other cases the divine communication is such as exceeds the power of human reason to discover; instances are the dreams of Abimelech (Gen. xx. 3, 6, 7), and especially those of Joseph (Gen. xxxvii. 5, xl. 3, xli. 1 f.). Other noteworthy instances of divinely sent dreams are Gen. xxviii. 12 ff., xxi. 24 ; Judges vii. 13 ; 1 Kings iii. 5 f.; Matt. i. 20, ii. 12 ff., xxvii. 19. E is specially fond of relating dreams.

The author of the speeches of Elihu also attaches

---

[1] חֲכִימִים   [2] חַרְטֻמַּיָּא   [3] *Supra*, p. 42 ff.

great importance to dreams as a channel of divine communications (Job xxxii. 14—16). It would seem that among many other resuscitations of primitive beliefs that of the symbolic character of dreams must be reckoned (cf. the dream-visions of Enoch, chs. 83—90, and the dreams in the Book of Daniel, also Josephus, B. J. ii. 7, 4 ; iii. 8, 13).

Naturally enough in the decay of genuine prophecy men looked about for artificial means of seeing future events. But the great prophets never refer to their dreams, and it is even a question how far all the visions of which they speak are to be taken literally.

HEBREW TERMS USED IN CONNECTION WITH DIVINATION.

The words which have to do with necromancy will be dealt with last of all, as they relate to divination by means of consultation with the dead.

(1) קֶסֶם (qesem) is the first and most important word to be considered. Though joining issue with Drs. W. R. Smith and Wellhausen as to its primary sense, there is no denying the fact that the connotation of the word is mostly got from divination. It is, in fact, the most general word for divination, and probably includes the rest. In Deut. xviii. 10 it stands before מְעוֹנֵן (me-'onen) and מְכַשֵּׁף (mekashshef), because including them, though W. R. Smith says it has the distinct sense of obtaining an oracle by drawing lots. In Ezek. xxi. 26 the word means casting lots by means of arrows, or perhaps mere rods. But in 1 Sam. xxviii. 8, Saul is made to ask the Witch of Endor to *divine* (קסומי ; Qeri, by an over-refinement reads קָסֳמִי) for him by means of the 'ōb (אוֹב).

It has been before remarked that the LXX. translators use for קוֹסֵם (qōsem) the quite general word μάντις.

In Hosea iv. 12 we seem to read of divination by arrows or rods, עֵץ apparently meaning the material, and מַקֵּל the form. Certainly those are wrong who see in עֵץ the אֲשֵׁרָה, for the reference is to some mode of obtaining an oracle, and not to worship.[1] It is almost certain that rabdomancy or belomancy is what Hosea refers to, and what Ezekiel (xxi. 21 ff.) describes. If, as seems likely, קסם is a general word, it would of course include the reference in Hosea. Taking it in its narrower sense, which R. Smith thinks original, it would be identical with what Hosea speaks of.

(2) מְעוֹנֵן (me'onen). Opinions differ widely as to the etymology and exact import of this word. (See Delitzsch on Isa. ii. 6.)

(i.) It has been said to be poel of a root עָנַן having the same meaning as גָּנַן and כָּנַן (كَنّ) "to cover." The מ" would then be "one who practises hidden or occult arts." But this meaning of עָנַן has no support in actual usage.

(ii.) More frequently and more plausibly it has been regarded as a denominative from עָנָן "cloud"; מְעוֹנֵן (or in its apocopated form עוֹנֵן) denoting one of two alternatives: either (a) one who observes the clouds with a view to obtaining an oracle. The ancients, we know, divined from the stars (see Daniel), the lightning (Iliad, ii. 353 ; Cicero, De Divin., i. 18 ; Pliny, ii. 43, 53), and also from the shapes made by the ever-shifting clouds (Joseph., Wars, vi. 5, 3). Or (b) the מְעוֹנֵן may be one

---

[1] Wellh. "Die Klein. Proph.," p. 108 f.

who brings clouds and storms (cf. Gen. ix. 14, "When I cloud clouds," i.e. bring clouds). That storms were believed to be raised by incantation is quite certain.[1]

The acceptation of this etymology and explanation would cause the word to rank with magical terms, and not with terms for divination. But there is nothing in the passages where the word is found to suggest that מְעוֹנֵן has anything to do with the sky; and it tells against it that the Hebrews seemed never greatly in danger of believing in astrology or practising it.

(iii.) By others מ has been made a denominative from עַיִן, and so עוֹנֵן is made to signify "to glance upon, to smite (with the evil eye)." This also would make the term a magical one.

But there is no other instance of such a form from a ע״י noun; and the Targum rejects this, for it renders by עַנֵּן "to practise sorcery," unless, indeed, it only transcribes the Hebrew word.

The LXX. represents the verb by οἰωνίζεσθαι, as in Num. xxiv. 1 it translates נְחָשִׁים by οἰωνοί. But this says little, as οἰωνός, though meaning strictly "a lone flying bird," came to be used among the Greeks for any omen. Examples of the practice of divining from the flight of birds are to be found in primitive Arabia.[2]

The word מְעוֹנֵן is usually translated by "observers" (Judges ix. 37, A.V. marg. "regarders") of times, A.V., or "augurs," R.V. (Deut. xviii. 10, 14; Lev. xix. 26; 2 Ki. xxi. 6). In Isa. ii. 6 and Micah v. 12, A.V. and R.V. "soothsayers" (so also Jer. xxvii. 9, R.V., where

---

[1] See Bernstein's "Syriac Chrestomathy," p. 111, line 9 f., and Wustenfeld's "Kaswini," i. p. 221, line 10 ff.

[2] See Wellh. Reste, p. 202 f.

A.V. has "enchanter"). Once the fem. sing. form of the word is Englished (both versions) by sorceress. An oak near Shechem, famous in divination, bears the name "Oak of Meo'nim" (Jud. ix. 37).

W. R. Smith follows Ewald[1] in tracing the word to the Semitic radix that exists in the Arabic غَنَّ (ghanna), to emit a hoarse, nasal sound. The מ they regard as one who speaks in a whispering, low tone.

In favour of the last explanation is the fact that low, nasal speaking attaches to several other terms used for magic and divination.

Apart from Fleischer's derivation of כָּשַׁף from كسف,[2] low, subdued speaking is implied in the Greek γόητης (see p. 71) and ἐπᾷειν, and in Isa. viii. 19 the אוֹבוֹת and the יִדְּעֹנִים are called whisperers (הַמְצַפְצְפִים), while in Isa. xxix. 4 it is said of Ariel, "And thou shalt be brought down ... and thy speech shall be low, out of the dust, and thy voice shall be as an 'ôb (אוֹב) : and thy speech shall whisper (יְתְצַפְצֵף) out of the ground."

3. נָחַשׁ. The verb נָחַשׁ is translated in the LXX. οἰωνίζομαι, which means, first to take omens from the flight and screams of birds, and then generally to forecast.

The Peshito version of Lev. xix. 26 adds to ܬܢܚܫܘܢ (Heb. תְנַחֲשׁוּ) the words ܒܟܗܐ ܚܘܬܐ, "by winged creatures" as an explanation, but this is due to LXX. influence.

In the Old Testament this mode of divination was practised on heights, as by Balaam, Num. xxiii. 3 ; pouring water into a cup was one of the ways by which

---

[1] "Die Lehre der Bibel von Gott," i. 234; cf. also Driver on Deut. xviii. 10. [2] *Supra*, p. 48.

it was done, as by Joseph, Gen. xliv. 5, 15. As regards the last, the practice referred to was that of putting water into a cup made of gold or of some other material. Then some precious stone was thrown in ; the rings formed on the surface were believed to predict the future. This is called in Greek κυλικομαντεία or ὑδρομαντεία (English, hydromancy). It was much practised in Egypt. (See authorities quoted by Dillman *in loco*.) For a parallel French superstition, see J. B. Thiers, " Traité des Superstitions," Paris, 1697, i. p. 187 ff.

Among the Arameans, omens of the נְחָשִׁים kinds were taken from the flight and cries of birds, from cries of beasts, from the conduct of fire, atmospheric changes—rain, etc.— and from the heavenly bodies. W. R. Smith [1] concludes, therefore, that this word includes all omens from natural signs. But he is too resolved to make words in Deut. xviii. 10, 11 have each a distinct sense. The author of Deut. and the people he wrote for were far from having that feeling of exactness which animates modern scholars.

In my treatment of לַחַשׁ I have already given my opinion that both לָחַשׁ and נָחַשׁ are denominatives from the noun נָחָשׁ (ל and נ interchanging).

Omens were certainly taken from the movements of serpents in early times.[2] Now just as in Greek οἰωνός, from denoting an omen from the flight of birds, came to mean any kind of omen, so נָחַשׁ acquired from the narrow sense of divining from serpents, that of divining from any sign (so Boch. Hiero. i. 20—21).

It is not at all impossible that the verb—still regarded as a denominative—means to hiss as a serpent, then to whisper. This would connect it with the many other

[1] Jour. Phil. xiv. 114 f.　　　[2] See Baud. " Studien," i. 157 ff.

magical and divinatory words which have such a connotation.[1] It would also confirm my belief that the magical is the primary signification of both לַחַשׁ (lakhash) and נָחַשׁ (nakhash).

4. גָּזְרִין (gazerīn) (emphatic form גָּזְרַיָּא) occurs in the sense of diviner in Aramaic only, and nowhere except in the Book of Daniel (ii. 27, iv. 4 [Eng. iv. 7], v. 7, 11, E. VV. soothsayers). The verb means " to cut, to determine " (cf. W. R. Smith's derivation of קְסַם [qasam] "to decide" from *first* meaning " to cut ") ; גְּזֵרָה (gazēra) " decree " also occurs in this book. The LXX. transcribes גָּזְרִין (gazerin) without attempting to translate. As these diviners are placed in Babylon, it is probable that astrologers are meant, though this is uncertain. Perhaps the word is to be understood like קֶסֶם (qesem), in a general sense. The Arabic root جزر (gazara) means to slaughter, and it may be that the גָּזְרִין originally offered a sacrifice in connection with their art. The Vulgate is probably wrong in rendering by " haruspices "; such omens are but once spoken of in the Bible (Ezek. xxi. 21)—a singular fact when one remembers how they bulk in other religions. In this one mention of this mode of divination it is a Babylonian, not a Hebrew practice.

5. אַשָּׁף (ashshaf) (Aram. אָשַׁף, ashaf) occurs in the Hebrew (i. 20, ii. 2) and Aramaic part (ii. 10) of Daniel, and nowhere else. As to its etymology, Praetorius, Fried. Delitzsch,[2] and Tallq.[3] agree that it is a Babylonian loan-word meaning magician, and especially exorcist. The verb in Assyrian is ašipu, the noun agent being eššipû. Delitzsch gives ašapû and ašipû (without dag.) respectively.

---

[1] See *supra* 81 and often. [2] " Proleg.," p. 141.
[3] " Assyr. Besch.," p. 20 and p. 158.

Accepting this, and remembering that the Book of Daniel, though written in Palestine about the middle of the second century B.C., is yet accommodated to the mode of thought and expression prevalent in Babylon, there is no good reason for doubting that the Hebrew and Aramaic word in Daniel has the same meaning as the Babylonian.

The LXX. renders אַשָּׁפִין (ashshaphin) by μάγοι, which to the Greek translators probably meant the same as the Assyrian word just given. Bevan (Com. on Daniel) is inclined to think that נזר, אשף and other terms found in "Daniel" were employed interchangeably, a supposition which is very unlikely to be correct.

6. כַּשְׂדָּאִים (kasdaim). This word stands correctly for the inhabitants of Babylon and its dependencies. It has this meaning from the establishment of the Neo-Babylonian Kingdom (see Jer. iii. 4, xxxii. 45; Hab. i. 6; Ezek. xxiii. 14, 15; Isa. xxiii. 13; xlviii. 14).

But in the Book of Daniel[1] the word seems to be synonymous with the caste of wise men. This sense the word got after the destruction of the Babylonian empire, and it is found in classical writers, to whom the only Chaldeans known were those belonging to this caste.

7. גַּד (Gad) and מְנִי (Meni). These are names of deities that were consulted with the view of securing a prosperous future. They were believed to be able to shape and to predict the future, so that they have a significance for divination; and as both are named in the Old Testament, it is well to take some notice of them.

In Gen. xxx. 11 the Qeri reads correctly בָּא גָד, "good

---

[1] i. 4; ii. 10; v. 7, 11.

luck comes "; so, too, the Pesh. and Targum. The LXX. (ἐν τύχη) and Vulgate (feliciter) follow the Kethib.

In Isa. lxv. 11 the word stands unquestionably for the Babylonian god of good fortune, identified with Bel, and later with the planet Jupiter. We can trace the name in בַּעַל גַּד (Josh. xi. 17) and in the Phoen. proper names נדעת, גדנעם.[1] Bar Hebraeus uses ܓܰܕܳܐ (gadda) in the sense of good luck.

מְנִי (Meni), mentioned in the same Isaiah passage, is another Babylonian deity, which had also to do with men's destiny. The author of the paragraph evidently accepts the derivation from מָנָה (minna) " to distribute, allot."

The LXX. translate by τύχη, as they do גַּד (gad) in the Genesis passage. It is singular that the Greek word τύχη stands for the Egyptian goddess Isis, which last is likewise the goddess of good luck. Perhaps Ištar, the Babylonian Isis, or moon god, is meant. Delitzsch (Franz) in his commentary, *in loco*, has surely gone wrong in identifying Meni with the Arabian Manât, one of the three principal pre-Islamic deities.

BIBLICAL NECROMANCY.

There remain to be considered terms or expressions which are used in the Old Testament to describe divination by consulting the dead. Three designations fall to be noticed, all of them found in Deut. xviii. 11.

(1) We shall begin with that which occurs last in the verse, viz. דֹּרֵשׁ אֶל הַמֵּתִים (one who inquires with [from] the dead) rendered by the A.V. and R.V. *necromancer*.

[1] See Eutung, "Sechs Phönizische Inschriften aus Idalion," 1873, p. 14.

Isa. viii. 19 makes it clear that this is a general description embracing the next two words to be considered. It is separately mentioned indeed, but the conjunction "waw" with which it is introduced is simply the explanatory "waw," answering to the Greek epexegetic καὶ. (See examples of this use of "wau" in Ges. Buhl, p. 197a, b.)

This phrase embraces the יִדְּעֹנִי (yidd°o'ni), and אוֹב ('ōb), and other kinds of necromancy. (So Driver on Deut. xviii. 11.)

(2) שֹׁאֵל אוֹב (sho'ēl 'ōb) one who consults an 'ōb. The word 'ōb is generally found with yidd°'oni. Like the last word, 'ōb, from meaning the spirit of a departed one, came to stand for the person who possessed such a spirit, and divines by its aid. The full phrase בַּעֲלַת אוֹב (the possessor of an 'ōb) is found in 1 Sam. xxviii. 7, where the "Witch of Endor" is so described.

The LXX. explains the word by ἐγγαστράμυθος, which means ventriloquist, i.e. one who made people believe that a ghost spoke through him by throwing his voice into the ground, where the spirit was supposed to be. This is the explanation of the phenomenon adopted by Lenormant,[1] Renan,[2] and by others. But the writer of Samuel, and other Biblical writers who speak of this species of divination, evidently regard it as really what it was claimed to be. Lev. xx. 27 is the only possible exception.

The etymology of the word is very uncertain. Passing by minor suggestions, the field seems to be held by two principal views. First, it has been traced to a root which means to return, which is found in the Arabic آوِب=أَوَب (aba=awaba). The word would in that case

---

[1] "La Divination," p. 161 ff.
[2] "History of People of Israel," i. 347.

mean the same as the French *revenant*, one who returns, i.e. the spirit who comes back. This derivation is defended by Stade (Gesch. Isr. i. p. 504), by Hitzig and Konig (on Is. viii. 19), and by Schwally (*Das Leben nach dem Tode*, p. 69); although now generally abandoned, it is at least as likely to be right as any other. Dr. Van Hoonecker (*Expository Times*, ix. 157 ff.) objects that in Deut. xviii. 11 the 'ōb is distinguished from the dead (metim); but if the latter clause of the verse is simply a generalization of the two foregoing clauses, this objection falls to the ground.

The commonest derivation is that which connects the word with 'ōb, "a bottle," literally something hollow. A similar word in Arabic وأب, (wa'ba) means a hole in a rock, a large and deep pit, i.e. as with bottle, something hollow.

Assuming the fundamental idea of hollowness to be in the word, many explanations have been suggested as arising out of it. I note two as being probably nearest the truth.

(1) Böttcher,[1] Kautsch,[2] and Dillmann[3] hold that the spirit is called 'ōb on account of the hollow tone of the voice; such a tone as might be expected to issue from an empty place. Other terms for practising magic and divination lend some support to this view.[4]

(2) The idea of hollowness has been held to apply in the first place to the cave or opening in the ground out of which the spirit speaks. Among the Greeks and Romans, oracles depending on necromancy were situated among large deep caverns which were supposed to communicate with the spirit world (cf. the Arabian

---

[1] "De Inferis," p. 101.   [2] Riehm, "Totenbesch."
[3] On Lev. x. 131.   [4] *Supra*, 81, 83, etc.

"Ahl al-ard" or earth-folk). W. R. Smith[1] was of opinion that divination by the 'ōb was connected with this superstition. Then just as 'ōb and yidd‘oni, from meaning spirit, came to stand for the person in whom the spirit dwelt, so by a similar metonymy—contained for container and *vice versâ*—the hollow cavern came to be used for the spirit that spoke out of it.

3. יִדְּעֹנִי (yidd‘oni). The English word wizard, by which this Hebrew term is rendered, means "one very wise," and agrees with the LXX. (γνώστης), Syriac (ܝܕܘܥܐ, yaddu‘a), Arabic (عَرّاف, ‘arraf), and with Ewald's rendering "Viel-wisserisch."

Like 'ōb, so also yidd‘oni, means in the first instance the spirit of a deceased person ; then it came to mean him or her that divines by such a spirit. W. R. Smith,[2] followed by Driver (on Deut. xviii. 11), distinguishes the two terms thus :—

Yidd‘oni is a familiar spirit, one known to him that consults it. The 'ōb is *any* ghost that is called up from the grave to answer questions put to it (cf. 1 Sam. xxviii). The yidd‘oni speaks through a personal medium : that is, through the person whom it possesses. The 'ōb speaks directly, as, for example, out of the grave (cf. 1 Sam. xxviii). Rashi (on Deut. xviii. 11) says that yidd‘oni differs from בַּעַל אוֹב (ba‘al 'ōb) in that he held in his mouth a bone, which uttered the oracle. It is hard to prove these distinctions to be either right or wrong, the data for forming a judgment are so slight.

But is it quite certain that the words are to be held as standing for distinct things ? Why may we not have in them different aspects of the same spirit ? So regarded,

---

[1] " Rel. Sem.," p. 198.   [2] Journ. Phil. xiv. 127.

'ōb would convey the notion that the spirit has returned from the other world, while yidd'ʻoni would suggest that the spirit so returned is knowing, and therefore able to answer the questions of the inquirer. The fact that in all the eleven instances of its occurrence yidd'ʻoni invariably follows 'ōb, is in favour of its being a mere interpretation. 'Ōb, on the other hand, is often found by itself (1 Sam. xxviii. 7, 8; 1 Chron. x. 3, etc.). I have already said that the expression at the end of Deut. xviii. 11 ("one who seeks unto the dead") is merely a generalized formula for the two foregoing characters. Now it is probable that these two characters are at bottom one, the "and" joining 'ōb and yidd'ʻoni in the way of a hendiadys: "he who seeks a departed spirit that is knowing." The remaining part of the verse is then simply a repetition in different words of the same thought. This is in complete harmony with the usages of Hebrew parallelism. The whole compound expression might be rendered as follows: "He who inquires of the departed spirit that is knowing, even he who seeks unto the dead."

Though condemned in the Old Testament,[1] necromancy held its own among the Israelites till a late period. Yahwism was opposed to both witchcraft and necromancy, yet the influence of habit and of intercourse with people around was too strong to be wholly overcome.[2] Winer[3] shows that in the ancient world, divination by calling back the spirits of the dead was very widespread among the Greeks, Romans, and other ancient nations. See the references he gives.

---

[1] See 1 Sam. xxviii. 7 ff.; Isa. viii. 19; cf. Lev. xix. 31, xx. 6, 27; Deut. xviii. 11.   [2] Schultz, ii. 322.   [3] "Totenbesch."

DIVINATION IN POST-BIBLICAL JUDAISM.

In the main the Talmud occupies the Old Testament antagonistic position regarding magic and divination.[1] Yet it is not wholly, and at times not at all, opposed to soothsaying; e.g. Khullin, 95b : יֵשׁ . . . נַחַשׁ שֶׁאֵין פִּי עַל אַף סִימָן "If (regarding a matter that is spoken of) there is no divination " נַחַשׁ, etc. Here there is not a syllable of condemnation about the נַחַשׁ. which is in the Old Testament uniformly reprobated. In Sanhed., 101a, even שֵׁדִים may be consulted if it is not the Sabbath. "On the Sabbath one may not put question to the שֵׁדִים " (i.e. on other days this may be done).

It should be remembered, however, that the Talmud is not one work composed by one author, and thus reflecting one mind. It is rather a repository of Jewish thought and folk-lore from the third to the seventh or eighth century of our era ; as such it is valuable, only we must not in it look for consistency.

DIVINATION AMONG THE ARABS.

Our principal sources of information on this subject are the works by Freytag[2] and Wellhausen[3] already named, and the authorities which they cite ; these last being mainly Arabic poetry, epic and lyrical.

There were both male and female fortune-tellers among the Arabs of the olden time, كَاهِن and كَاهِنَة being the respective terms employed. There can be no doubt that كَاهِن is identical with Heb. כֹּהֵן, and that in both the

---

[1] See Khullin, 7b ; Sanhed., 67b.   [2] "Einleitung."
[3] "Reste."

magician or priest and the soothsayer were joined.
حَاجِب properly door-keeper (i.e. one who had charge of
the temple entrance) and سَادِن (one who ministered at
the qaaba) were the words used for the priests, and when
this office was rigidly separated from the other, the
distinction consisted in the fact that the priesthood was
hereditary and was exercised at the temple, while the
office of soothsayer opened itself to anyone qualified by
special inspiration to discharge it.[1]

As to the vexed question of the etymology of كَاهِن and
כֹּהֵן I must content myself by a reference to the authorities named by Gesenius-Buhl.

The Arab soothsayer was called also حَازِ or حَزَّاء (which
is the same root as the Hebrew חֹזֶה), though the latter
is specially used of an astrologer, and the former of one
who divines from moles on the face and the like.

Other words are نَائِف (pl. نَافَة), which means especially
weather prophets and palmists,[2] and عَرَّاف literally a
knowing one (the form فَعَّال denoting office or occupation).

The communications of the Arab soothsayers were
given in rhythmical form, which, however, was largely
due to the character of the language they spoke in.

Among well-known soothsayers the following are
named by either Freytag[3] or Wellhausen[4]:—Satbih, of
the tribe of Dsib; Shiqq of Bagila; Aus b. Rabi'a; Al-
Khims of Taghlib; Amru b. Algu'aid; Ibn Kajad of
Medina, while Tsuraifa and Sagah were women.

---

[1] See Wellh. "Reste," p. 134, and W. R. Smith, Journ. of Phil.,
xiii. p. 278.

[2] See Sharastani's "Book of Religions and Philosophical Sects," ed.
Cureton, ii. p. 437.   [3] p. 157.   [4] "Reste," p. 136 f.

MODES OF DIVINATION.

These Arab soothsayers took omens from the flight of birds, from writing made on the ground, from the human body—especially the face, from the lines on the hand (palmistry), and by watching the descent of balls which had been thrown into the air. For technical words and expressions for these see Freytag.[1]

PRESAGES.

There were certain phenomena which were interpreted as signs of either good or evil. The approach of a raven was an intimation that friends were to be separated. Hence the proverb : أَشْأَمُ مِنْ غُرَابِ الْبَيْنِ, " Unluckier than the raven of separation."

The bird called أَخْيَلُ (the green woodpecker probably) was also looked upon as presaging evil (طِيَرَة), as contrasted with فَأْل which was a good omen.

ISLAM AND DIVINATION.

It has already been stated [2] that although Mohammed condemned divination, he was himself too superstitious to entirely dispense with it. Yet his general attitude towards it was hostile.

Mu'awiyah ibn Hakam relates that he asked the Prophet if it were right to consult fortune-tellers about future events, and he replied, " Since you have embraced Islam you must not consult them." [3]

Qaṭ'an ibn Qabīsah says : " The Prophet forbade

[1] p. 158 f.   [2] *Supra*, p. 22.   [3] Hughes, p. 130a.

taking omens from the running of animals, the flight of birds, and from throwing pebbles, which were (was) done by the idolaters of Arabia." [1]

For some time after Mohammed's death many arose in Islam who claimed in the manner of the كَاهِن to forecast the future. But their number soon declined, owing mostly to the acceptance of complete monotheism, the authority of the Quran and the traditions of the Prophet.

The Moslem doctors say that up to the time of Jesus the Jinns had liberty to enter any of the seven heavens. With His birth they were excluded from three of them. Mohammed's birth caused them to be shut out of the remaining four. Yet even afterwards they continued to ascend the boundaries of the first heaven, and could hear the angels converse of God's decrees. In this way they obtained a knowledge of the future, which under certain conditions they imparted to men.

BABYLONIAN AND ASSYRIAN DIVINATION.

The diviner among these peoples was called *bârû*, seer, from *bârû* to see. Compare with this the Hebrew רֹאֶה and the more poetical חֹזֶה, Biblical terms for "prophet," both denoting literally "seer." The office of diviner among the Babylonians and Assyrians was called *bârûtu*, a word denoting literally the "act of seeing," cf. the corresponding abstract Hebrew term חָזוּת. The *bârû*, like the *eššepu*, belonged to a priestly caste, his special function being that of prognostication. The signs or omens were of the kind common among

---

[1] Mishkât, Book xxi. 2, quoted by Hughes, p. 114b.

Greeks, Romans, Arabs, etc.; full descriptions of these are found on the clay tablets discovered among the ruins of Nineveh. These tablets formed part of the library of Assurbanipal, the last of the Assyrian kings. Among these omens may be mentioned the cries and flight of birds, the movements of animals, dreams, and, especially, the position and motions of the heavenly bodies. Astrology is generally believed to have taken its rise among the Babylonians. However uncertain this may be, its prevalence in Babylon from the earliest historical times is not to be questioned. Next in importance to observation of the heavenly bodies, dreams were consulted by the *bârû.* Assyrian kings and generals were often guided in their policy by divination. We have an instructive example in Ezek. xxi., where King Esarhaddon takes omens from the fall of arrows and from the liver of animals offered in sacrifice. For further and fuller details, see Lenormant's "La Divination," etc., and A. Bouché Leclerq's "Histoire de la Divination dans l'Antiquité."

Egyptian Divination.

The newest book discussing divination as it prevailed among the Egyptians is Wiedemann's already referred to. I can do no more here than refer to p. 261 ff. of this work for a treatment of the subject.

III. DEMONOLOGY.

THE belief in evil spirits is universal. As to its origin, I must refer to remarks made at the outset.[1]

Polyanimism—if the word is to be tolerated—is the precursor of polytheism, as this last is itself the precursor of dualism in the first instance and then of monotheism. In all this we have in action the scientific and philosophic principles of reducing the many to the one.

As showing how widespread the belief in evil spirits is, I may name the following works (see full titles at the commencement—Literature): Among the Chinese, Dennys and Nevius; among the Dravidians, etc., in India, Caldwell; among the Arabs, Freytag's "Einleitung" and Wellhausen's "Reste"; among the Singalese, see *Journal of the Ceylon Branch of the Royal Asiatic Society*, 1865-6, "Demon Possession." Dr. Roskoff's "Geschichte des Teufels" gives a mass of information as to the prevalence among all peoples of dualism in religion.

DEMONOLOGY IN THE OLD TESTAMENT.

Notwithstanding the fact that the Old Testament as a whole stands opposed to the belief in evil spirits, yet

---

[1] See *supra*, p. 8 ff. It is doubtful, and even more than doubtful, whether in the strict sense devil-worship exists or has ever existed. What is so called, is probably nothing more than prayer and sacrifices to well-disposed spiritual beings with the view of securing the help of these last against spiritual beings which are malicious.

there are many indications and survivals throughout the Old Testament of this superstition.

Firstly, many demons are referred to by name: שֵׁדִים, in Deut. xxxii. 17, and in Ps. cvi. 37 are demons; שְׂעִירִים, literally, "hairy ones," are goat-like demons which dwelt in the wilderness,[1] Isa. xiii. 21 ; xxxiv. 14, etc.

עֲזָאזֵל, Lev. xvi. 8, 10, 26, is a demon that had its home in the wilderness, though both Mishna and Gemara explain it as a steep rock over which the goat was hurled.[2]

לִילִית (Assyrian Lelitu, also masc. Lêlu) was a night ghost (לַיְלָה, or is this a mere popular etymology ?) or demon, Isa. xxxiv. 14, 4.[3]

The רְפָאִים are spirits who dwelt especially in Sheol, but they also roam about on the earth, where they once lived.[4]

עֲלוּקָה in Prov. xxx. 15, rendered by the LXX. βδέλλη, Vulg. *sanguisuga*, and in the English versions "*horse-leach*," is probably a vampire or blood-sucking demon. Thus Mühlau de Prov. Aquri, 42 ff., and Wellhausen "Reste," 149.

In Arabic the word for horse-leach is علق, while عُلَّق, formed from the same root "to hang," means the kind of Jinn called Ghoul (غُول).

Reference has been more than once made to the serpent as a demon. In Ps. lviii. 5, פֶּתֶן seems to be

---

[1] See W. R. Smith, "Rel. Sem.," p. 423 ; Wellh., Reste, p. 151 L. Cf. the Teutonic representation of the Devil as a he-goat (Grimm, p. 995).   [2] Joel i. p. 63.

[3] See Grünbaum, Z.D.M.G., xxxi., p. 250, f.; Baethgen's "Sindban," p. 8 f. ; Wellh., Reste, p. 150 ; W. R. Smith, "Rel. Sem.," p. 423 ; and Cheyne on Isa. xxxiv. 14.

[4] Wellh., Reste, p. 150, and his "Israel. und Jüd. Gesch.," p. 99.

regarded as an evil spirit against whom binding charms are applied.

In the Talmud[1] and by Rashi,[2] the בַּעַל אוֹב is called a Pithom (פִּיתוֹם), one who has his head resting on his breast between his two shoulders, and utters his oracle from his armpits ; or, probably, simply with hands raised and his head lying between both armpits. The word is surely from the Biblical פֶּתֶן, " adder," and is connected with the Greek πύθων, which means first a serpent, then a soothsayer. The Talmudic פִּיתוֹם would appear to be one that summoned the serpent demon to give an oracle. But the exact meaning of the Talmud is a mystery.

The Hebrew Môt (מוֹת), Duma (דּוּמָה), and Sh°ol (שְׁאוֹל), were originally demons or Jinns, corresponding to the Greek Κὴρ, Θάνατος and Ἀιδης, and to the Roman Lethum, Mors and Pluto.

According to Philo of Byblus († end of first century A.D.) Môt was the son of El. Phœnician and Jewish traditions say he hovered near dying persons. The name occurs in צַלְמָוֶת restored by Nöldeke to its old etymology of צַל and מָוֶת (see Z. A. W., 1897, p. 183 ff.), and אֲחִימוֹת ; cf. name Mutaddu in the Tel-el-Amarna tablets; and the modern river name Nahr-el-Mût (Baedeker's " Palestine ").

The Jewish Aggada says that Duma (דּוּמָה, silence) is the name of the angel of death. There is a tribe on the Syrian boundary that bears this name. Perhaps it was the name of the totem animal first of all ; then the name of the tribe devoted to this animal.

---

[1] Sanhed., 65a, b.   [2] Comm. on Deut. xviii. 11.

There is a town in the Haurân of the same name, and another among the mountains of Judæa between Hebron and Beersheba; modern name ed-Dauma. Sh'ol (שְׁאוֹל), now a synonym for grave קֶבֶר, was originally a spirit presiding over the underworld, answering to the Pluto of Roman mythology.

Thus Môt, Dumah and Darkness in the folk-lore of the Hebrews were demons; not, however, indeed exclusively in the bad sense we attach to that word, for they were regarded as to some extent friendly.

In Exodus iv. 24 we read that Jehovah met Moses and sought to kill him; through the circumcision of his son Moses was let alone. This has been explained as meaning that an evil spirit laid hold of Moses, and that the circumcision of the child caused it to depart.

Sober exegesis is against this, but it is a fact that circumcision has been regarded as a protection against demons; the child, up to the time when the ceremony took place, being considered to be under demoniacal control. Just as in the early Church, at the ceremony of baptism, a formula of exorcism was uttered by the officiating minister, as is done at the present time in the Russian orthodox Roman Catholic and German Evangelical Churches. Indeed, infant baptism not improbably originated in the view that until baptism everyone was in the power and Kingdom of Satan.

Eisenmenger [1] gives proof that among the Jews circumcision was believed to give efficacy to prayer. After circumcision, prayer was heard, though previously it might not have been heard.

The ear-rings which Jacob buried under the oak of

---

[1] "Jud. Ent.," i. p. 682 f.

Shechem were (as remarked before, see p. 52 f.) amulets.[1]
These ear-rings are thus explained by Kleinert in Riehm
("Zauberei"), Delitzsch (Franz. Comment. *in loco*), W. R.
Smith (Journ. Phil. xiv. 122) and Smend, p. 126, cf.
Wellhausen, "Reste," p. 165, note 6.

The שַׂהֲרֹנִים or moonlets, were moon-shaped amulets
worn around the neck by men and women, and
even put on camels. (See Judges viii. 21 and 26;
Isaiah iii. 18.)

Wellhausen,[2] Dozy,[3] give هلال as an ornament. The
Greeks used to adorn themselves with inscribed
sunlets and moonlets.[4] The modern horseshoe often
hung up in houses, is a survival of this amulet.

Israel is urged in Hos. ii. 2, under the figure of the
wife of the prophet, to put away her whoredoms *from
her face* (פָּנִים) : (i.e. the nose-ring which was a charm
against the evil eye), and her adulteries from *between
her breasts* (i.e. necklaces, also worn as amulets). These
nose-rings and necklaces, when worn, meant an acknowledgment of the heathen religion, in which they were
considered to protect against the evil eye.

The serpent in the history of the fall is a form of the
demon.[5]

The bells (פַּעֲמֹנִים Exod. xxviii. 33 f., xxxix. 25 f.)
which hung from the high priest's garment, were in the
first instance amulets to frighten the evil spirits away.
It is a fact that from very ancient times, storms, rain,
thunder, lightning, hail, etc., were ascribed to demons.[6]
Burton in his "Anatomy of Melancholy," p. 123, says

---

[1] See Gen. xxxv. 4 ff.   [2] "Reste," p. 165.
[3] Dozy, Lexicon, *sub voce*.   [4] See Jahn, p. 42.
[5] See Smend, 119; cf. Wellh., Reste, p. 152 ff.
[6] Crooke, i. 65.

that "sudden whirlwinds, tempestuous storms," though often referred by meteorologists to natural causes, are most frequently due to " aerial devils."[1]

Among the East Indians, the storm-bringing demons are scared away by any kind of noise, and especially by that of sounding metal. The Circassians sprinkled holy water over their friends' graves, and the priests tolled bells near them, in order to keep evil spirits away.[2]

In Pegu, copper vessels or bells were used to frighten away demons that wished to disturb the repose of the dead.[2]

Rabbi Bachia b. Asher (Saratoga, 1291), in his " Commentary on the Pentateuch," is quoted by Ennemoser[3] as saying that when interments took place a boy stood near the middle of the body, ringing a bell that the evil spirits might be kept at a distance.[4]

It is now generally held that the object of the ringing of the bells in the דְּבִיר of the Temple was that the people outside might know the exact moment when the priest entered the most holy place.[5] It is quite possible, notwithstanding its magical origin, that it came to have this function.

DEMONOLOGY IN THE APOCRYPHA.

The Old Testament Apocrypha is comparatively free from direct allusions to demons and their work.

We have, however, an important exception in the book of Tobit, chapters vi. and vii. Tobias, son of Tobit,

[1] Cf. Tylor, ii. 26.   [2] Grant, p. 276.   [3] i. p. 380.
[4] Cf. Tylor, ii. p. 113.
[5] See Exod. xxviii. 35 ; cf. Eccles. xlix. 5, and Luke i. 9, 21.

is sent under the guidance of the unknown angel
Raphael to Ecbatana, to claim money due to his father,
and to seek for himself the hand of Sarah, the beautiful
daughter of Raguel who lives in that city. In the
Tigris, a fish is caught, of which he is told, by his angel
guide, to reserve the heart, liver, and gall ; the first two
are to prevent the demons, who had killed the former
husband of Sarah, from killing Tobias the first night of
his marriage. This turns out exactly as intimated at
the time of the catching of the fish. Sarah is so loved
by a powerful demon, that seven men who had in turn
married her were by him put to death the night of the
marriage, before indeed it was consummated.

But the heart and liver of the above fish saved the
life of Tobias ; by means of them the devil is driven into
Egypt (viii. 1—3).

The demon referred to before is called Asmodeus, and
the incident shows that at the time when the book was
written (some time in the second century B.C., according to Fritzsche, Bissell and Rosenmann) demons were
believed to be capable of sexual love, reminding one of
the love of the sons of God for the daughters of men in
Gen. vi. 2, and especially of the Jinns among the Arabs,
whom W. R. Smith [1] rightly regards as by no means
peculiar to the Arabs, though the name probably is.

Two opinions prevail as to the etymology of the name
Asmodeus. A Semitic origin is claimed by the Talmud
(in which he is called מֶלֶךְ הַשֵּׁרִים), and by several modern
scholars.

The root would in that case be שׁמד, which in Hiph.
means to destroy, Asmodeus being an aphel form. But for

[1] "Rel. Sem.," p. 422.

noun agent, " destroyer," we should, had this etymology been correct, have had Masmodeus, not Asmodeus.

The great bulk of modern scholars identify this Asmodeus with the Persian Ashma, who in the Avesta is next to Angromainyus, the chief of the evil spirits. Benfey, Stern, Windischmann, Fritzsche (in Schenkel *sub voce*) and Kohut, say the word means covetous, lustful. The last part of the word is, they say, derived from doeva (div)=demon (cf. θαῖος, deus).   Thus also Baudissen (Herzog ii.).

Rev. J. M. Fuller,[1] while admitting the Persian origin, holds that the character given to Asmodeus agrees with Babylonian rather than with Persian belief.

Evil spirits are referred to in some other parts of the Apocrypha—such as in Wisdom ii. 24 (" by the envy of the devil [ὁ διάβολος] death entered into the world ").   In Ecclus. xxi. 27 Satan is mentioned.

DEMONOLOGY IN THE NEW TESTAMENT.

Those miracles recorded in the Gospels by which demons were expelled, show that in the time of Christ the belief in demoniacal possession and in the power of exorcism was prevalent among the Jews.   It has been the habit among Christian expositors to accept these accounts in their literal sense.   Thus Edersheim,[2] Delitzsch,[3] Rev. Walter Scott,[4] and the bulk of theological writers, not to mention the widespread belief of the Churches.

This same belief prevails among the Chinese at the present time.   Dr. Nevius, for many years an American

---

[1] Speaker's Commentary.   [2] " Life and Times of the Messiah."
[3] In Riehm, art. " Besessene," i. p. 209b.
[4] " The Existence of Evil Spirits."

Presbyterian missionary in China, says that the modern Chinese have the very same conceptions, as to possession and exorcism, which the Jews entertained in the first century of our era. Moreover, he contends that, though when he first settled in the country he strongly opposed these conceptions, he adopted them subsequently as his own.

Rev. R. Bruce, B.A., at present a missionary in the same country, told me some months back (February, 1897) that a prominent convert to Christianity had, before his conversion, a great reputation as an exorcist. People supposed to be possessed came or were brought to him from all parts. Notwithstanding the fact that he has ceased to belong to the popular religion, and, indeed, is now an eloquent Christian preacher, yet the natives, though not themselves Christians, continue to flock to him, and he is, they say, as successful now as before his change of religion.

Mr. Bruce tells me that the Chinese converts to Christianity take the gospel narratives concerning demon possession quite literally, and the missionaries do not feel called upon to correct the views they have, even if they hold different views from the natives.

There can, however, be no doubt that in all these cases, in Palestine and in China, nothing more is meant than certain diseases superstitiously regarded as due to demoniacal influence.

Among the Jews of a later time, and probably at this very time, שֵׁדִים or demons are designated according to the diseases they induce. There were demons of asthma, croup, hydrophobia, insanity and indigestion.[1]

[1] See authorities quoted by Edersheim, ii. p. 759.

How widespread this view is, appears from what Dr. E. B. Tylor tells us of the Indian Archipelago and its superstitions.[1]

It is a confirmation of the identity of demons and diseases that among all peoples the favourite resorts of demons are damp places, latrines, ovens, ruined houses, rivers, etc., in the East the most prolific originators of sickness.

Tallqvist[2] says that among the Assyrians, demons were named after the diseases due to them. He further tells us that the connection was so close that names of demons and corresponding diseases came to be identical.

Demons were among the later Jews supposed to be capable of being transferred from one individual to another, or from human beings to animals. We come across this formula in the Talmud : " May the blindness of M, the son of N, leave him and pierce the eyeballs of this dog."[3]

D'Alviella[4] speaks of the same idea—that demons were transferred from human beings to animals, stones, etc.

Compare with this Christ's casting out of demons from the man on the east of the Sea of Galilee, and causing them to enter swine in such wise that the swine rushed into the lake and were drowned (Matt. viii. 28 f.; Mark v. 1 ff.; Luke viii. 26 f.; cf. also Mark vi. 25).

Josephus, who was born less than a decade after the death of Jesus, has an interesting parallel to this. In Antiq. viii. 2, 5, he gives an account of a celebrated exorcist of his time, by name Eliezar. He saw him, not only casting out evil spirits, but giving ocular demonstration of

---

[1] " Prim. Cult.," ii. 127.   [2] " Assyr. Besch.," p. 17.
[3] Gittin, iv. 66.   [4] Hibb. Lect., p. 88 f.

the fact. This Eliezar proceeded thus—and all this the Jewish historian says he "saw with his own eyes." He applied to the nostrils of the possessed a ring having attached to it a root which Solomon is made to have prescribed. The demons came out through the same nostrils by which they are alleged to have entered. This last is significant, for how many diseases are traceable to what is inhaled. As the demons came out, Eliezar caused them to pass into a basin filled with water, which was at once thrown over.

The same superstition as to the connection of demons and disease obtained among the Egyptians, as I have already pointed out.[1]

We have before us in the New Testament, phenomena which are upon all fours with what we see among the best known nations of antiquity, and there is no doubt that in all cases we have the same data—disease due to demoniacal influence, and recovery a result of driving out the demon. This is not the place to vindicate the character of Christ in either winking at the ignorance or superstition of His contemporaries, or in being Himself the victim of such ignorance or superstition. This is the task of the theologian, and I do not think it is a very difficult one. I will, however, say this much, that we do not read of Christ's employing such means as exorcists employ. He never counsels the wearing of amulets. He appears even to despise those who do put on such defences as phylacteries, etc. He applies no medicament; He utters no incantation; He simply speaks the word.

In Acts xix. we have two noteworthy incidents. In

---

[1] See Wiedemann, p. 271 ff.

verse 12 we are told that not only was Paul able to cast out demons and heal diseases, but that handkerchiefs and aprons which had been in contact with his body had this same power. This is much like the anti-demoniacal magic which one meets among heathen nations.

In verses 13—20, many of those at Ephesus, who practised " curious," i.e. " magical " arts (περίεργα), brought their books together and burned them in the sight of all. We know from other sources, literary and monu-mental, that the Ephesians used such written charms, called ἐφέσια γράμματα.

The formulæ were written on leather generally, though some on papyrus, on lead, and even on gold. Those mentioned in the present instance must have been more valuable than leather. They could hardly have cost £2000 (50,000 drachmas) unless some were made of gold. Such charms have been dug up from the ruins of Ephesus.

ANTICHRIST.

It appears to me that the Antichrist legend, the seeds of which are to be found in Daniel, where Antiochus Epiphanes is the arch-enemy of God, is part of the same general conception.

In later Judaism the Antichrist appears as Armillus, under which name he often figures in the Jewish fables of the Middle Ages. He is known by this name already in the Targum of Jonathan on Isaiah xi. 4.

In 2 Thess. ii. 1—12, and in Rev. xiii. 20, this concep-tion comes prominently forward. Whoever is meant— and emperors, popes, and many others have been put

forward—it appears to me that we have here the operation of that dualism which was so powerful a factor
in the Oriental world, and especially among the Babylonians and Persians. It is a pity that Bible expounders
so generally regard the conception as a product of the
Jewish mind alone. It is really part of a very general
idea among Eastern peoples.

A short and simple account of views respecting " Antichrist," or its equivalent in the Bible and among Jews
and Christians in later time, may be seen in Findlay's
excellent Commentary on " the Epistles to the Thessalonians," p. 170 ff. But for a full history of the " Antichrist Legend," students will consult the able work of
Bousset (Englished by A. H. Keane, London, 1896).

Demonology of Josephus.

The great Jewish historian, Josephus, was born A.D. 37
and died A.D. 100, i.e. so near the time of Jesus Christ
that his belief may be regarded as sampling the Jewish
beliefs of Christ's day.

In Antiq. viii. 2, 5, already referred to, he says that
God taught Solomon how demons were to be expelled,
a " science useful and sanitative to men." He (Solomon)
composed incantations by which demons were exorcised
and diseases healed.

The " root " by which Eliezar drove out evil spirits is
very like, if not identical with, that which he describes
in Wars, vii. 6, 3. He calls it " Baaras," probably the
Hebrew בֹּעֲרָא boara, burning, for he describes it as
flame-like in colour, emitting at evening a lightning-like
ray. Unless protected by certain drugs, it is fatal to
touch it. It must also be carried in a certain way. All

this shows how closely in the mind of Josephus, as in all times and among all peoples, demonology and magic go hand in hand, this last supplying the antidote to the former.

DEMONOLOGY OF THE PSEUDEPIGRAPHICAL WRITINGS.

The word Pseudepigrapha (ψευδεπίγραφα) is used by many Protestant scholars to designate a number of Greek writings, called mostly after patriarchs, prophets etc., of the Old Testament, such as Enoch, Testament of the Twelve Patriarchs, Psalms of Solomon, etc. By far the most important of this collection for our purpose is the Book of Enoch, and we shall refer to no other.

In chs. vi.—xvi., which belong to the ground-work of our existing Book of Enoch, and which Charles dates before B.C. 170, we have a history of the fall of the angels. This came through their lusting after the daughters of men, whom they at length marry, and from whom they get children. These children are giants in strength and their wickedness proportionate.

Demons, according to ch. xvi. 1, are the ghosts of those malicious giants gotten of the angels by the daughters of men. These demons, in their disembodied state, are allowed to bring moral ruin among men until the time of the final judgment.

In ch. liv. 6 and ch. lxix. 5, which, according to Charles, is eighty or ninety years later than the other part, Satan is set forth as the ruler of a counter kingdom of evil, though one subject to the Lord of spirits. He it was who led the angels astray, and made them subjects of his kingdom.

DEMONOLOGY IN POST-BIBLICAL JUDAISM.

The Mishna and Talmud fall first to be considered, and this can be done but briefly.

It is indisputable that, as compared with the Gemara, the Mishna is very free from magic and demonology. The reason for this is not far to seek.[1]

The Mishna is almost wholly halachic, i.e. it contains for the most part laws for the government of Jewish persons, homes and communities.

Then, again, it was conceived and put to writing[2] at a period when Jews were very exclusive. In later times the Jews settled numerously in Babylon, Persia and Egypt, and contact with other religions would make them broader, and more ready to adopt new principles and practices.

There are, however, in the Mishna, as Joel is compelled to admit, undoubted traces of magic. (See Joel i. p. 57.)

But it is in the Gemara that demonology and magic bulk largely; and it is particularly interesting to note that what in the Mishna has a natural explanation, is regarded in the Gemara from the magical point of view.

עַיִן הָרַע in the Mishna means simply " envy," as in Pirqe Abot ii. 11 : " Envy (עַיִן הָרַע), evil desire, and

---

[1] See *supra*, 61 f.

[2] Whether the Mishna was ever, as such, put to writing prior to or even during the time of the Amoraim is uncertain. The Amoraim simply quote the tradition ; no MS. of the Mishna is once referred to in either Talmud. Yet it is hardly likely that such an immense collection of material should be handed on by word of mouth alone. It has been said that for each part of the Mishna separate scholars were set apart. When, therefore, in the schools of Surah, Pumbadith, Tiberias, etc., the sections of the Mishna were discussed, the text was supplied by the persons appointed to commit the particular part to memory.

hatred of human creatures, take men out of the world."
Cf. v. 19: "Envy (עַיִן הָרָע), and haughtiness and lust."

In these passages the effect is taken for the cause, just
as among the Assyrians and in later Jewish literature,
demons and diseases are identified.

We have in the same tract of the Mishna[1] the
antithetic phrase עַיִן טוֹבָה, which must have been formed
by analogy.

In the Talmud, and in other Jewish writings of a later
time, עַיִן means "a sickness due to the action of demons."
See Levy, *sub* עַיִן, for examples.

Magic and demonology reached their highest point
among the Amoraim in the time of Abaya (best known of
the Pumbaditha teachers) and Raba, who was head of
the Machusa Rabbinical school.

Abaya acknowledges that he had changed his own
opinion as to demoniacal influence.   Thus he says,[2]
formerly he looked upon washing of the hands after
meals as needful for cleanliness only ; but later he came
to believe it to be necessary in order to remove all traces
of contact by evil spirits.   Formerly the sin of eating out
of a bundle of vegetables consisted in the fact that it
showed greediness.   But subsequently he came to see
that such a bundle contained an evil spirit, and each part
taken out of the bundle was injurious for that reason.

Joel, in Heft i. and ii., gives detailed accounts with
adequate citations of the magical and demonological
beliefs and practices which prevailed among the Jews
from the time of the Gemara to comparatively modern
times.   See also Brecher's compact and interesting book.

I submit here a brief and general statement concerning

[1] ii. 9.   [2] Khullin, 105b.

Jewish demonology. In this part I am much indebted
to Weber and to Kohut. Full references to authorities
are given by these writers.

Evil spirits are called mazziqin (מַזִּיקִין), i.e. beings who
injure (נזק). They are divided into two main classes:—

I. Fallen angels who are wholly supernatural. Their
leader is Satan, a spirit of delusion (רוּחַ הַשְׂטוּת), an
accuser (מְקַטְרֵג κατήγορος), and the messenger of death
(מַלְאַךְ מוֹתָא). (See Kohut, p. 88-9.) He is not to be
distinguished, Weber thinks, from Sammael (סַמָּאֵל,
the poison of God, i.e. a great poison), who was once an
archangel near the throne of God. He it was who in
the form of the serpent deceived Eve (Weber 253).

II. The second class of מַזִּיקִין (mazziqin) are half
supernatural and half human. Of these note two
separate kinds :

(1) The לִילִין (cf. לַיְל "night") Lilin, begotten of
Adam on the one side, and Lilith and other female
spirits on the other. Lilith reigns over these as queen.

(2) The שֵׁדִים (שׁוּד "to be violent") Shedim, the
offspring of Eve and male spirits. Their king is Asmedai
(=Asmodeus), who, however, resembles the merry if also
mischief-making hobgoblins of fairy tales,[1] more than he
does the Persian Asmai or the Apocryphal Asmodeus
(though these last two are not quite identical).

In the time of Solomon all these demons existed and
practised their arts. He, however, so long as he kept
the commandments of God, had absolute control over

[1] Cf. the German *Zwerge*. See Grimm's "Teutonic Mythology,"
1409 and 1861.

them, their leaders as well.   But as soon as he fell into sin, the demons were *his* master and not he *theirs*.[1]

These demons, as the corresponding beings among Arabs (Jinns) and Assyrians, carried on their work in the night.   The moment the cock crew their work was gone (Weber 255).   Has the incident about Peter's denying Christ before the cock crowing any reminiscence of this ? (cf. Matt. xxvi. 75).

COUNTERCHARMS.

Among the Jews the methods of self-protection against demon agency were similar to those in vogue among other nations, Arabs, etc.   These consisted of amulets, incantations and physical agents.

Phylacteries (תְּפִלִּין), mezuzas (מְזוּזוֹת), and tsitsith (צִיצִת) were at the first charms against demons, though Weber (p. 27 f.) denies this, maintaining with most modern Jews that their purpose was at the first to remind those who wore tefillin and tsitsith, and those who passed through the doors, of their duty to love and serve Jehovah.

But according to M⁰nakhot, 33b and Berishit Rabba, ch. 35, the mezuza served to protect the house against injury.   R. Elieser b. Jacob, in M⁰nakhot, 33b, says, " Whoever has the tefillin on his head, the mezuza on his door, and the tsitsith on his mantle, may feel sure that he cannot sin, for it is said, Qohel. iv. 12, ' a threefold cord is not easily broken.' "   Weber explains the impossibility of sinning on religious grounds—the power of the tefillin etc., to keep the commands of Jehovah in

[1] See Kohut, p. 81 f., and Grünbaum, Z.D.M.G., xxxi. p. 204.

remembrance. But the quotation shows that it is a magical binding that is meant.[1]

Weber gives quotations from Jewish writings (Talmud, etc.) to show that the religious explanation was the true one. But all that he succeeds in showing is that there were in early times, Jewish scholars who endeavoured to explain these charms in a rational way, and this either for the sake of vindicating Judaism from the calumniations of Christians, or in order to supply a rational basis for these primitive superstitions, which are to be found in our own time among the Jews of all countries. Modern Jews will often wear tifillin and tsitsith as they go about, believing them to prevent accidents, sickness and death. In December, 1887, I travelled from Alexandria to Jaffa in a steamer in company with a Jew who wore his tifillin the whole journey. But while we reached Palestine in safety, the tifillin did not keep off from either him or me the demon of sea-sickness.

Other safeguards were the pronunciation of the Aaronic blessing,[2] of the "Sh⁰ma'"[3] and its accompanying prayers, and of passages of Scripture which had power under special circumstances. Thus, if the traveller recited Zech. iii. 2,[4] he could keep away the angel of death. If Psalm xcj. was said before the sleeper closed his eyes, he would be sure to awake safely in the morning. Upon waking, he was not to rub his eyes until he had washed them, lest the בַּת חֹרִין (demon of sickness) should blind him.

---

[1] See Targum on Cant. viii. 3. W. Robertson Smith (Journ. Phil., xiii. 286) says, " the phylacteries are survivals of old superstition."
[2] Num. vi. 24—26.   [3] Deut. vi. 4—9.
[4] " Jehovah said unto Satan, ' Jehovah rebuke thee,' " etc.

Fumigation was another device employed (cf. Tobit vi. 16, viii. 3). Perhaps the smoke of the fish's liver in Tobit was believed by its offensiveness to drive away the demon, just as the sweet-smelling odour [1] served to attract Jehovah.

Demons were supposed to feed on certain particles at night. It was therefore dangerous to drink water in the night lest Shabriri (שַׁבְרִירִי), the demon of blindness, should smite the drinker.[2] The latter might, however, cause the demon to gradually decay by lopping off the syllables of his name one by one and pronouncing the continually shortening name. Thus *Shabriri, briri, riri, ri*. Directly the drinker said *ri* the demon died. This answers to what is now called sympathetic magic.

Sources of Jewish Magic and Demonology.

Two main views have been held as to the principal quarter from which Judaism was influenced in its magical and demonological beliefs.

On the one hand, Persia with its Zoroastrianism is claimed as the chief factor. On the other, Babylon and contiguous Aramaic countries are pointed to as that.

The first view is defended with considerable learning and with great vehemence by two Jewish Rabbis, Kohut and Schorr.

The second and more recent view is advocated by Lenormant,[3] and by Dr. Gaster,[4] the last making Gnosticism the immediate and Babylonianism the ultimate factor.

---

[1] רִיחַ נִיחֹחַ, Lev. i. 9, and often.   [2] Abodah Zarah, 12b.
[3] "Chaldean Magic."   [4] *Asiatic Journal*, Jan., 1896.

Schorr's first volume appeared before Kohut's, and he probably suggested to the latter some points, and perhaps the drift of his argument. But his second Heft came out in 1872 ; i.e. six years after Kohut's book was published. Schorr's special aim was to show that the Talmud is of little worth, as it owes nearly all it contains to other religions and especially to Parseeism. In his second work he charges Kohut with gross inaccuracies, alleging that he did not understand the Talmud. He is profoundly surprised that the German Oriental Society (D.M.G.) should have issued with its imprimatur so unscientific a production. Prior to this, however, Kohut had in the *Nachtrag* of his work[1] made an attack upon Schorr.

There are in Kohut's work many blunders which ordinary care could have prevented. Thus at p. 33 he translates מַר as a proper name, and has therefore to insert *Gott* to make a subject for the following verb.

Mar is not a Jewish doctor as Kohut assumes, but simply a name of God—" The Lord stretched forth His hand."

For his acquaintance with Zoroastrianism the author is indebted, as he acknowledges, to the writings of Sprenger and Windischmann, which he constantly cites.

He thinks he has proved his thesis when he has shown that there are resemblances between post-exilic Judaism and Parseeism. This is therefore the task he sets himself to accomplish, and in this he succeeds, as it was easy to succeed. But Kohut shows no knowledge of the Babylonian religion, from which Parseeism borrowed its most essential doctrines, and to which scholars are more and

---

[1] p. 96, ff.

more disposed to trace the magic and demonology of later Judaism.

Kohut says, that although Jews were transplanted to Mesopotamia and Babylon, many of them crossed over to Persia. According to Esther iii. 8, Jews dwelt in all the provinces of Persia. Josephus[1] says the Jews were carried by Nebuchadnezzar to Media and to Persia : further on[2] in the same work he says, many of the Jewish exiles had passed from Assyria to Persia.[3]

Granting all this, it is nevertheless true that the majority of Jews remained in Mesopotamia and Babylon, and it is much more likely that they were influenced by the religions of these countries.

Kohut cannot resist the temptation to quote Isa. xlv. 7[4] as showing Persian influence. But fire or light was worshipped among the Accadians long before we read of it among the Persians. From the Accadians it passed to the Babylonians, who took over, not only the country, but the Cuneiform mode of writing and much of the religion. From the Babylonians it was received by the Zoroastrians.

Lenormant[5] and Tallqvist[6] show the importance of the fire-god (cf. the Agni of the Vedas). Dr. Friederich Jeremias says that Gibil, the Babylonian fire-god, was undoubtedly the most powerful deity invoked by the exorcist.[7]

So likewise dualism was rife among the Accadians and Babylonians as well as among the Persians, though they

---

[1] Antiqq. ix. 15.   [2] xi. 52.   [3] Kohut, p. 4 f.
[4] "I form the light and create darkness. I make peace and create evil."
[5] "Chald. Magic," p. 184 f.   [6] "Assyr. Besch.," p. 23.
[7] De la Saussaye, i. p. 214.

had not reached the two unities which the Parsees had worked to, Ahuramazda and Agromainyus. Lenormant[1] holds, however, that the Babylonians had a clear conception of the divine unity, notwithstanding their apparent Pantheism and Polytheism.

It is important to note that for seven or eight hundred years after the Exile, the Jews show scant traces of the alleged Parsee influence. The doctrine of Satan in Job, Zech. etc., of the good and bad angels of Ezek. ix. 2—4, of the archangels Gabriel and Michael—these might just as well have come by way of Babylon.

Kohut[2] tries to show that Gabriel is the counterpart of the Zoroastrian Çraosho. But Lenormant[3] points out that Çraosho is taken from the Accadian Silikmulukhi. It is possible, in general, when Kohut finds in Parseeism parallels to Old Testament angelology or demonology, to find such parallels in the Babylonian and often in the Accadian religion.

Kohut thinks the principle of arranging angels in orders, archangels (Michael and Gabriel) and angels, is a sign of contact with Persia. But Lenormant[4] says that among the spirits believed in by the Accadians there were such hierarchical ranks.

It is in the period subsequent to the second century of our era that Judaism shows the most remarkable development in regard to angelology, demonology and magic. It is not therefore so much a question as to what people influenced the Jews during the Exile, but rather who influenced them most during the Talmudic period. The Amoraim had schools in Palestine (Tiberias, Sepphoris, Cæsarea and Lydda) and in Babylon

---

[1] "Chald. Magic," p. 112.
[3] "Chald. Magic," p. 195.
[2] p. 28.
[4] Ib., p. 24 f.

(Neharda, Sura, Pumpaditha, Mahusa and Neresh) ; but those of Babylon were the largest, drew the best teachers, and they lasted the longest.

Anz.[1] has shown that the Babylonian religion continued to flourish until the second century of our era at least ; and traces of Gnosticism can be found in the very first centuries, if not, indeed, in the time before our era set in. When the ancient religion of Babylon ceased to exist as an institution, its dogmas did not cease to be known or even believed ; nor did they cease to be operative upon the forces of heathenism, Judaism and Christianity, with which they came in contact.

In Zoroastrianism, which it always modified in the Jewish schools of the country, and in the Talmud which preserves their teaching, we have the continued life of the old religion of the Accadians.

It may be said that Zoroastrianism was the immediate factor that operated upon Babylonian Judaism ; but even this is not to be conceded, for there were in Babylonia at this time Gnostic sects which inherited and handed on, much of the old national religion.

It is being more and more acknowledged that Judaism owed much, if not most, of its magic to Gnostic influence. (See Gaster, p. 152 f.) It is only now getting to be seen how deep and widespread was the power wielded by Ophites, Mandæans and other Gnostic sects.

The mystic magic of the Qabbalah is certainly due to this influence.

Prof. Kessler[2] and Ans—the latter with much learning —show that Gnosticism, heathen, Jewish and Christian,

---

[1] "Zur Frage" etc., p. 60 f.

[2] Encyc. Brit. "Mandæans": Herzog—Plitt "Mandäer" ; cf. also his "Ueber Gnosis und Altbabylonische Religion" in Transactions Berlin Oriental Congress, 1882.

has its roots in the ancient religion of Babylon. The Mandæans exist at the present time, and have been visited in recent years by the late Dr. Petermann and by Prof. Dr. A. Socin.

Gunkel says,[1] "The more Babylonianism becomes known to us, the clearer does it get that it operated powerfully in very late post-Christian times. Babylonian elements are to be traced among Hellenistic Greeks. Gnosticism and, later, Manichæism as well as Madaism, have preserved in them considerable elements of Babylonian tradition."

The late Principal Tullock[2] defends the old view that Gnosticism was indebted principally to the theology of Alexandria (Philoh), and especially to Parseeism.

The discovery and interpretation of Cuneiform monuments and careful study of Eastern religions, is proving that it has been the habit to over-estimate the influence of Parseeism in shaping Judaism, and to under-estimate that of Babylon.

It would be wrong, however, to deny that Persian religion did have some formative power upon both Babylonianism and upon Judaism.

Joel differs from his brother Rabbi in that he attaches more weight to the Babylonian than to the Persian influence.[3]

DEMONOLOGY AMONG THE ARABS AND MOSLEMS.

Freytag[4] and Wellhausen[5] are our principal authorities on this subject. Lane in his "Thousand and one

---

[1] "Schöffung und Chaos," p. 294.   [2] Encyc. Brit. "Gnosticism."
[3] Professor Cheyne's "Jewish Religious Life after the Exile" has come into my hands as I am correcting the final proofs. I am glad to see that he attaches greater importance to Babylonian than to Persian influence. (See p. 25 ff.)
[4] "Einleitung," p. 164 ff.   [5] "Reste," p. 148 ff.

Nights "[1] and in his "Modern Egyptians," has a long and valuable note on "Jinns." This Hughes has epitomized and somewhat adapted in his dictionary under "Genii." Goldziher [2] gives some valuable notes on the subject.

The Jinns of the Arabs are not to be considered as demons *sui generis*, as seems to be implied by many writers. This has been rightly emphasized by W. R. Smith.[3]

Yet the name is peculiar to the Arabs, for the derivation from the classical Genii, or the identifying of the roots, has been rejected by all modern Arabicists. In the first edition of his " Reste " Wellhausen contended that Jinn was a loan-word; Nöldeke [4] showed, on the contrary, that it is a genuine Arabic word, and in the new edition of his " Reste "[5] Wellhausen very candidly acknowledges Nöldeke's correction to be just, and he accordingly adopts it. Its strict meaning is " covering," " hiding " it being the noun of action of the verb جنّ. Then from its abstract meaning it acquires the concrete meaning of those who hide themselves, or who dwell in secret places. الْجَوَالى is also a term used for the Jinns.

جانّ the participle of the same verb is another designation of the Jinns. But Arabian writers are not consistent in their use of this word, as sometimes it stands for Iblis, the father and ruler of the Jinns, while at other times it is used interchangeably with Jinn (جنّ). See Lane's note.

Islamic writers distinguish between angels (مَلَائِك)—all of whom are good, devils (شَيَاطِين)—all of whom are bad, and Jinns (جنّ), some of whom are good and some bad.

---

[1] Ch. i., note 21.   [2] " Abhand." i.   [3] "Rel. Sem.," p. 424.
[4] Z.D.M.G., xli. p. 717 ff.   [5] p. 148, note 3.

In Quran lxxii. 11 the Jinns are made to say "some of us are good and some otherwise" (نُوَنَ ذٰلِكَ) : this last meaning the antithesis to good—bad, though the commentator Zamakshari takes the sense of the last clause to be intermediate between good and bad.

The demons of Islam were, for the most part, gods worshipped in the "time of ignorance," just as the prophets of Yahwe reduced heathen deities to the same level.[1]   Quzaḥ (قُزَح) the pre-Islamic god was to the Moslems a Satan or Jinn.[2]

This accounts for the important fact rightly emphasized by Wellhausen[3] that the Jinns so commonly assume a serpent form.   Indeed, the words jānn (جانّ) and ghoul (غُولٌ) became names for the serpent.

Among other names of Jinns the following may be given :—*Male* : Ifrit (عِفْريت) ; Azabb (أَزَبّ), literally hairy, cf. Hebrew שָׂעִיר) ; Izb (أَزِب) ; Aziab (أَزْيَاب).   *Female* : Ghul (غُولٌ); 'Aulaq (عَوْلَق); Alūq (عَلُوقٌ=Heb. עֲלוּקָה in Prov. xxx. 15).   Freytag (p. 167) adds several others to this list.   خابِل, literally "corrupter," is used for Jinn and devil.

Several attempts have been made to differentiate between the functions of these several evil spirits.[4]

In the Quran, Sur. 55, the inhabitants of the earth are represented as of two kinds, men and demons.   In verse 31 ثَقَلَن literally "two heavy ones," or weights, i.e. two bodies of creatures is used to describe them.

Among the Moslems the word Satan came to be used

[1] See *supra*, p. 38.   [2] Goldziher, "Abh.," p. 112 f.
[3] "Reste," p. 152.   [4] See Lane's note, and Freytag, p. 167.

in the same sense as Jinn. Hence we have in the Quran [1] the plural Satans (شياطين), and the activity ascribed to these Satans is of a piece with what is elsewhere said of the Jinns.

Mohammed showed his usual diplomacy in accepting the heathen belief in Jinns, though in a modified form. In the Quran,[2] in the Hadeth, in the life of the Prophet by Ibn Ishām, and in other quarters, Mohammed's doctrine of Jinns is more or less fully spoken of.

In the opening of Sura 72 are these words : " Say, it hath been revealed to me that a company of Jinns listened, and said : ' Verily we have heard a marvellous discourse ' " (Quran). Here the Prophet clearly assumes the real existence of the Jinns.

But what the Prophet strongly reprobated was the heathen practice of *worshipping* the Jinns.

Musejlima and the false prophet al-Aswad al 'Ansi, too, were acknowledged to be under the influence of Jinns. What of truth the كاهن predicted was by Mohammed ascribed to the fact that it came from the Jinns.

Even the Mu'tasiliten, who professed to contend for pure and unadulterated Islam, assumed the Jinns to have a real existence.

Moslem philosophers were disposed to minimize the *rôle* played by demons. Neither al-Farabi, the Arab Aristotle (†950), nor Masa'udi (†956), denied the existence of Jinns. Abu Sina (Avicenna †1037) was the first Moslem writer of note who relegated the Jinns to the realm of mere fable. On the relation of Islam to the doctrine of Jinns, see Goldziher, 107 ff., and Sprenger's

---

[1] vi. 70 ; xxiii. 99 ; xxxviii. 36.   [2] xxxvii. 8 ; lxxii. 9, etc.

" Leben und Lehre des Mohammads," ii. pp. 239—251, quoted by Goldziher.

The English " Will o' the Wisp," or " Jack o' lanthern," was supposed by the early Arabs as by our European forefathers, to be carried by Jinns. Indeed. similar beliefs are still to be met with in our own country. Among the pre-Islamic and Islamic Arabs the Jinns were commonly conceived of as carrying with them lights,[1] and also as riding on animals, especially the fox.[2] It will be of interest in this connection to note the divine appearance to Moses in the burning bush (Exodus iii. 2).

Location.—They dwell specially in sandy barren deserts (براص, sing. برصّة) unapproachable to man, such as Abgar, Barahut, Baqqâr, Tsaihad and Jabrin. Really, however, these spots are magic oases in such deserts. But the tame and friendly Jinns are not seldom denizens in the homes of human beings. They are to be found in large numbers among the mountains of Qaf (قاف) which surround this world. They live, too, in holy trees, and in damp, dark places of the earth ; in fact, they may be found anywhere.

Time of Action.—It is in the night they carry on their work.

Form.—Though their proper and distinct form is that of the serpent,[3] they can assume any form at will, animal or human. But they are generally invisible, and it is the *work* not the *worker* that is to be seen. If a man or woman disappear in the wilderness, it is at once put down to the Jinns who have carried them off. Any abnormal, unexplainable event is credited to them.

---

[1] See Goldziher, " Abh.," p. 20.   [2] Ib., p. 209.
[3] Wellh. Reste, p. 152 f.   W. Robertson Smith, however, denies this, see " Rel. Semites," p. 422.

Indeed they are a kind of *deus ex machina* to account for what else would be unaccountable, this suggesting a possible cause of their being so largely believed in by the curious Arabs.

Work.—Accidents, sickness, insanity (hence called جنون), the inspiration of singers, of poets, and of prophets —these and much else are ascribed to Jinns. They often post themselves at windows and on roofs, and throw large stones at people who pass by. They steal clothes, food, etc., and when anything is missing they are often blamed for the theft—a boon for the real thief!

Mode of Life.—The Jinns eat and drink like other people. They are male and female, marry and get children. Sometimes they have children by human beings, the offspring partaking of the nature of both parents. Some Jinns are peaceable and friendly, others the reverse. Like men, they are divided into believers and unbelievers. Those who are good Moslems discharge the duties of religion—prayer, alms, fasting during the month Ramadân, the pilgrimage to Mekka and Mount Arafât, with as much care as the most devoted among believing men.

As among later Jews, so among Moslems, Solomon plays an important part in reference to the Jinns. The means by which he was able to control them was a most beautiful sealing-ring, which he received direct from heaven, and on which was engraved the "great name" of God (الأسم الأعظم). By virtue of this ring Solomon was able to compel the Jinns to assist in building the temple of Jerusalem.

Lane[1] gives a sketch of some spirits generally believed to be an inferior kind of Jinn. Among these he names the Ghūl, Si'lat or Si'la, Ghaddâr, Dalhân and Shiqq.

[1] " Arab. Nights," i. p. 36 ff.

COUNTERCHARMS.

(See also "Magic among the Arabs," p. 63 ff.)

These, in the main, are of the usual kind: amulets, material agents and formulæ of incantation, showing that we are dealing with a general superstition and not with anything that was confined to the Arabs, though there are in all such cases peculiarities due to physical environment, temperament, and religion.

Among *amulets* may be mentioned rings suspended from the ears and nose and worn on the fingers. Bands and girdles were worn, much as the modern Jew carries under his clothing the Talith Qaton [1] (טַלִּית קָטֹן).

Among physical agents the plant called حَرْمَل was believed to act as a deterrent to demons. Citron in the house kept demons away.

Incantations were also used. Among the Moslems these were parts of the Quran and other religious formulæ. The "spell" called رُقْيَة, consisted of a string of passages from the Quran. The same passages could be written on an amulet.

ASSYRIAN DEMONOLOGY.

Under the head of "Assyrian Magic," [2] much was of necessity said that forms part of demonology.

To the innumerable company of demons belong the seven evil spirits whose names and full character are unknown; the depths of whose nature have never been

---

[1] A small garment worn next the skin, covering the breast. It answers to the large garment (Talith Gadōl) worn in the synagogue. Both have at the corners the tassels (צִיצִית), wrongly translated "hems" in the Eng. versions.

[2] See *supra*, p. 67.

fathomed in heaven or on earth. But there is an innumerable company in addition to these seven.

They work evil upon human beings either of their own free will on their own account, or by command of the gods, who use them to execute vengeance upon the wicked.

They sow the seeds of discord in family life. They cause the most attached friends and even lovers to detest each other. To bring about strife, quarrels and wars, is their delight. There is no disease which they may not induce. Sickness, calamity, sudden death, these and all nameable and even conceivable ills they produce and promote.

They accomplish their nefarious ends in ways similar to those rampant among the Jinns or demons of other nations : such as the evil eye, the magic word, by breath and by spittle.

They can be overcome and their work undone with the help of the supreme deities, and especially by that of the Magic Trinity, Ea, Marduk and Gibil. In this we have nothing really unique, though among the Babylonians the intervention of favourable spirits, or, if you will, deities, is made particularly prominent.

But either implicitly or explicitly all efforts to frustrate the activity of evil spirits involve the good offices of friendly ones. In all magic and demonology whether among savages or among civilized people, there is implied a dualism of good and evil—the counterpart and reflex of what is seen in human life. The modern science of comparative religion will render good service by showing the sameness, or, at any rate, the similarity of the principles underlying magic and demonology in all ages and climes.

COUNTERCHARMS.

These are much the same as those we have had to look at as obtaining among Hebrews, Arabs and others.

We have, as preventives, amulets, incantations and material agents.

Incantations are said, but in Assyria as in Egypt it is the priests who, in the main, recite them. Each disease, each demon-caused evil has its peculiar formulæ, and it required much training to know which to employ. Besides, in both countries the *mode* of repeating the charms—generally in a low, gurgling monotone—was of great moment.

Physical agents bulk largely in Assyrian demonology. Many were really medicinal, and had their origin in their healing character, though ostensibly they were efficient because anti-demoniacal. In line with what we now call sympathetic magic,[1] fruits, animals, etc., were burnt, and as these disappeared in smoke and flame the ills also vanished. It is quite open to conjecture that these holocausts of fruits, animals, etc., had a sacrificial origin, though the conception connected with images of demons (see below) favours our regarding them as a part of sympathetic magic.

If, as noted before,[2] an image of a demon was made, to injure and even to destroy the image was to bring a corresponding fate upon the demon whose image this was.

The material of which the image was made varied according to the locality and the means of the person who wished to punish the demon in question. Wood, wax, clay, were among the ingredients used.

[1] See Jevons, p. 28 ff., and *supra*, p. 17 f.   [2] See *supra*, p. 69.

EGYPTIAN DEMONOLOGY.

The Egyptians had their gods whom they worshipped, and whom they invoked against the demons. For a succinct and up-to-date account of the Egyptian deities, see Wiedemann, p. 103 ff.

But they believed equally in demons whose power is exercised in this world and in the next.

Among this people, as among the Assyrians, the friendly and hostile deities are sharply distinguished, and in this case, too, magic is but the employment of appropriate means to bring the influence of the friendly deities to bear against the hostile ones.

It is characteristic of Egyptian magic and demonology that they busied themselves very much with the affairs of the future life. This could hardly be otherwise with a people in whose religion the doctrine of a life to come constituted a very vital part.

Demons were believed by the Egyptians, as by others, to bring about sickness, death, and all sorts of misfortunes. Diseases were particularly thought to be their work, as I have more than once had to notice. Magic and medicine were therefore inseparably combined.

COUNTERCHARMS.

These are, as before, amulets, incantations and material agents.

As regards amulets, they were of various kinds and worn on the bodies of all sorts and conditions of men. Moreover, when buried with a dead body they were supposed to secure safe entrance into the fruitful fields where Osiris reigns, and protection during the subsequent life there.

Wiedemann[1] gives a full account of the amulets used by the Egyptians for the dead and for the living.

Incantations were also used. When a body was being embalmed, and afterwards when it was interred, sundry formulæ were pronounced, generally by the priests.

Much importance was attached to the way in which the incantations were said. If beautifully uttered and repeated with sufficient frequency, these incantations possessed unlimited power. But the very conditions demanded, wherever possible, the services of a priest. Indeed prayer among the Egyptians was almost exclusively magical, i.e. its efficacy resided in the manner in which it was said, and not in its contents, and still less in subjective or ethical conditions.

PHŒNICIAN AND SYRIAN MAGIC AND DEMONOLOGY.

Little has been written on the prevalence and character of magic and demonology among these peoples. In the work of De la Saussaye, which deals briefly with the religions of the Syrians and Phœnicians, nothing is said of magic and related subjects.

These peoples were in religious matters less original than the Hebrews, the Assyrians, the Egyptians, or the Arabs, and they have left fewer and less important remains, literary or monumental, than the other nations named.

We know, however, that the Syrians believed in demons, and practised magic even after they embraced Christianity. The Syriac legends of Tur Abdin collected by Prym and Socin are important as showing this. (See index, " Dämonen, etc.")

[1] p. 284 ff.

K

Wellhausen[1] refers to the legend that Simon Stylite banished from the land of Lebanon demons and wild beasts.

Rev. G. Margoliouth, M.A., Keeper of Oriental MSS. in the British Museum, tells me there is but one Syriac MS. in the Museum containing magical charms in Syriac. Two or three years ago two others were offered for sale to the Museum, but were refused. The Rev. H. Gollanz, M.A., of the Battersea Synagogue, London, purchased and has since made a translation of them. This translation he is about to publish in the transactions of some learned society. These MSS. are, however, small and rather modern. In January, 1897, I was permitted to see both the MSS., and also the translation.

Mention may be made of the inscribed cups and bowls from ancient Babylon with Aramaic inscriptions.

---

[1] " Reste," p. 152, note 2.

VITA.

Ich, Thomas Witton Davies, wurde am 28sten Februar 1851, in Stadt Nantyglo, Grafschaft Monmouthshire, Gross Britannien, geboren. Als Knabe und als Jüngling besuchte ich zuerst die " National Schools " zu Witton Park, in Grafschaft Durham, und nachher die " British Schools " zu Escomb, in derselben Grafschaft.

Von August 1872 bis Mai 1877 studierte ich Mathematik, die classischen Sprachen, Philosophie und Theologie im " Baptist " Kollegium, damals zu Pontypool, jetzt zu Cardiff gelegen.

Die nächsten zwei Jahre besuchte ich folgende " Colleges " in London : " Regent's Park College," " University College," " New College," " Manchester New College."

Im Juni 1878 verlieh mir das " University College " London, den ersten Preis (Prize) in Logik, Ethik und Psychologie, und in October 1879 erwarb ich mir den Grad eines B.A. von der Londoner Universität durch die vorschriftsmässigen Prüfungen.

Nachdem ich hierauf von November 1879 bis December 1880 Pastor zu Merthyr Tydfil gewesen war, wurde ich im December 1880 gewählt als Professor der classischen Sprachen und des Hebräischen in dem " Baptist College," Haverfordwest; in welcher Stellung ich bis December 1891 blieb.

Innerhalb dieser Zeit (October 1881) unterzog ich

mich der "Hebrew and Scripture Examination" der Londoner Universität, deren Fächer folgende waren: Hebräischer Text des Alten Testaments ; Griechischer Text des Neuen Testaments ; Biblische Geschichte und Kritik nebst Apologetik. Ich bestand mit Auszeichnung, und erhielt den Preis der "Ersten Klasse." Endlich legte ich im October 1883 die "Further Hebrew and Scripture Examination" derselben Universität mit Erfolg ab.

Seit Januar 1892 bin ich "Principal" und Professor der Theologie im "Midland Baptist College," Nottingham ; seit vier Jahren gleichzeitig Professor des Alten Testaments im "Congregational Institute," Nottingham, sowie auch seit 1896 "Lecturer" in Arabisch und Syrisch im "University College," Nottingham.

Ueber meinen Studiengang habe ich ausser dem bereits Gesagten noch zu bemerken, dass ich während des Sommers 1886 auf "Queen's College," Oxford, Unterricht bei Professor A. H. Sayce, M.A., LL.D., nahm : ferner im Sommer-Semester 1892 mich an der Berliner Universität immatriculiren liess, wo ich die Herren Professoren Barth, Dieterici, Dillmann, Sachau und Strack und den Doctor Winckler hörte, und dass ich im April 1897 nach Leipzig kam, um hier die Herren Professoren und Docenten Buhl, Dalman (Delitzschianum), Socin, Schwarz und Stumme zu hören.

Ergebenst,

THOMAS WITTON DAVIES.

Leipzig, Carolinen Strasse, 13 Ggbde.,
    21. *Juni* 1897.

New and
Forthcoming Books

Published by

James Clarke & Co.,

13 & 14, Fleet Street,

London.

October, 1898.

13 & 14, FLEET STREET,
LONDON.

October, 1898.

James Clarke & Co.'s
New and Forthcoming Books.

~~~~~~~~~~~~~~~

Fiction.

J. Bloun-delle Burton.

THE SCOURGE OF GOD: A Romance of Religious Persecution.

By **John Bloundelle-Burton,** Author of "Across the Salt Seas," "The Clash of Arms," "In the Day of Adversity," &c. Crown 8vo, cloth, 6s.

Pictures of Lancashire Life.

John Ack-worth.

THE SCOWCROFT CRITICS.

By **John Ackworth,** Author of "Clog-shop Chronicles" and "Beckside Lights." Crown 8vo, art linen, gilt top, 3s. 6d.

"Clog-shop Chronicles" is now in its Ninth Thousand.

New Work by Marianne Farningham.

Marianne Farningham.

A PARIS WINDOW: A Romance of the days of the Franco-German War. Based upon fact.

By **Marianne Farningham.** Crown 8vo, cloth, 5s.

The Story falls in the days of the Siege of Paris and the Commune, and is based on materials gathered from those who lived through that awful time.

———

New Uniform Edition of Emma Jane Worboise's Novels.

Emma Jane Worboise.

OVERDALE: the Story of a Pervert.

By **Emma Jane Worboise.** Crown 8vo, gilt top, art linen, 3s. 6d.

ST. BEETHA'S; or, the Heiress of Arne.

By **Emma Jane Worboise.** Crown 8vo, gilt top, art linen, 3s. 6d.

JOAN CARISBROKE.

By **Emma Jane Worboise.** Crown 8vo, gilt top, art linen, 3s. 6d.

GREY AND GOLD.

By **Emma Jane Worboise.** Crown 8vo, gilt top, art linen, 3s. 6d.

These are the first volumes of a New Uniform Edition of the Novels of Emma Jane Worboise. They are entirely reset in new type, printed on a specially-made paper, and bound uniformly in a crimson art-linen, with gilt tops.

A Devonshire Story.

Mary Hartier.

CHAPEL FOLK.

By **Mary Hartier.** Crown 8vo, cloth, 3s. 6d.

———

Small Books on Great Subjects.

New Volumes.

Stopford A. Brooke.

THE SHIP OF THE SOUL, And Other Papers.

By **Stopford A. Brooke, M.A.** Pott 8vo, buckram, 1s. 6d. [*November.*

R. J. Campbell.

THE MAKING OF AN APOSTLE.

By **R. J. Campbell,** of Brighton. Pott 8vo, buckram, 1s. 6d. [*October.*

R. F. Horton.

THE CONQUERED WORLD, And Other Papers. [*Ready.*

By **Robert F. Horton, M.A., D.D.** Pott 8vo, buckram, 1s. 6d.

———

For Christmas and the New Year.

Geo. Matheson.

THE BIBLE DEFINITION OF RELIGION.

By **George Matheson, M.A., D.D.,** Senior Minister of the Parish of St. Bernard's, Edinburgh. On deccle-edge paper, with red border-lines and decorated wrapper, in envelope, suitable for use as a Christmas and New Year greeting. Price 1s.

C. Silvester Horne.

A Gift-book for the Sorrowing.

THE ORDEAL OF FAITH.

By **C. Silvester Horne, M.A.** Meditations on the Book of Job, designed as a "ministry of consolation to some who are pierced with many sorrows." Fcap. 8vo, handsomely bound in cloth, gilt top, 2s. 6d.

———

J. E. Ritchie.

New Book by Christopher Crayon.

CHRISTOPHER CRAYON'S RECOLLECTIONS: The Life and Times of the late **James Ewing Ritchie** as Told by Himself. With Portrait. Cr. 8vo, cloth, 3s. 6d.

———

T. Witton Davies.

MAGIC, DIVINATION AND DEMONOLOGY AMONG THE HEBREWS AND THEIR NEIGHBOURS, Including an Examination of Biblical References and of the Biblical Terms.

By **T. Witton Davies, B.A., Ph.D.,** Lecturer in Semitic Languages, University College, Bangor, and Professor of Old Testament Literature at the Bangor Baptist College. Crown 8vo, cloth, 3s. 6d.

———

N. Fox.

CHRIST IN THE DAILY MEAL, or the Ordinance of the Breaking of Bread.

By **Norman Fox, D.D.** Cr. 8vo, 3s.

Introduced by the RIGHT HON. JAMES BRYCE, M.P.

L. W. Bacon.
J. Bryce.

A HISTORY OF AMERICAN CHRISTIANITY.

By **L. W. Bacon**, with Introduction by the Right. Hon. **James Bryce**, M.P. Crown 8vo, cloth.

———

A. H. Moncur Sime.

THE LITERARY LIFE OF EDINBURGH.

By **A. H. Moncur Sime.** Pott 8vo, cloth, 1s.

Dr. GEORGE MATHESON says :—"*I am simply charmed with your historical sketch. It presents in terse and vigorous language, and with graphic power of delineation, a picture which in the space of half-an-hour will make the citizen of the modern Athens master of the literary history of Edinburgh, and which every Edinburgh citizen ought to buy. A brochure like this makes the mouth water; it awakens my thirst for a literary Home Rule in Scotland such as we had in the days of* THE EDINBURGH REVIEW."

Sir LEWIS MORRIS says :—"*It is a very intellectual sketch of the life of the Northern capital, and contains much that will be fresh to most readers. The style is bright throughout and very pleasing.*"

"*While brief, it is not scrappy, and conveys a great deal of information in a very agreeable way.*"—ABERDEEN FREE PRESS.

"*Mr. Sime shows that he knows his facts, and has given thought to them.*"—SCOTSMAN.

"*A well-written outline of a quaint and fascinating subject.*"—THE LITERARY WORLD.

"*A brief but luminous sketch.*"—THE SPEAKER.

"*An agreeable little book.*"—LITERATURE.

The Polychrome Bible.

Paul Haupt, H. Howard Furness.

A New English Translation of the Books of the Bible. Printed in Colours exhibiting the Composite Structure of the Books. With Explanatory Notes and Pictorial Illustrations from Nature and from Ancient Monuments of Egypt, Assyria, Palestine, &c. Prepared by Eminent Biblical Scholars of Europe and America, and edited with the assistance of **Horace Howard Furness**, by **Paul Haupt**, Johns Hopkins University, Baltimore.

Volumes Ready or Nearly Ready :—

C. J. Ball

THE BOOK OF GENESIS. Translated, with Notes, by **C. J. Ball**, **M.A.**, Chaplain of Lincoln's Inn, Editor of the " Variorum Apocrypha."   [*May, 1899.*

H. E. Ryle.

THE BOOK OF EXODUS. Translated, with Notes, by **Herbert E. Ryle**, **D.D.**, President of Queen's College, Cambridge, and Hulsean Professor of Divinity.

S. R. Driver, H. A. White.

THE BOOK OF LEVITICUS. Translated, with Notes, by **S. R. Driver**, **D.D.**, Regius Professor of Hebrew and Canon of Christ Church, Oxford, one of the Revisers of the Authorised Version, and **H. A. White**, **M.A.**, Fellow of New College, Oxford. 114 pp., printed in two colours (55 pp. translation, 50 pp. notes). Four full-page illustrations (one in colours), and

S. R.
Driver,
H. A.
White.

four illustrations in the Notes. Cloth,
gilt top, price 6s. net. [*Ready*.

"*Leviticus has fared badly. It has been regarded
either as a mass of uninteresting and obsolete ritual
or as a quarry for incredible allegorising. Driver
and White have rescued it from the double reproach.
It is a book of genuine historical and religious
worth, and every chapter overflows with interest.
They simply restored it as it is. And it is most
precious and stimulating. There is little variety of
colouring of course, but the translation is beyond
anything yet done into English, and the notes are
full and pertinent. There are four full-page plates
and four smaller illustrations.*"
—EXPOSITORY TIMES.

"*A version that will make the sense of the original
more clearly intelligible to the English reader than
any existing version. . . . The notes as a whole
are admirable; it would be difficult, and even impossible, for the English reader to find elsewhere in any
convenient form such help in the interpretation of
Leviticus.*"
—G. BUCHANAN GRAY IN "THE CHRISTIAN WORLD."

"*The names of the translators, Canon Driver and
Mr. H. A. White, are ample guarantees for the high
scholarship and critical soundness of the work. The
translation is, it is hardly necessary to say, exact.
It may be more to the purpose to add that it is
also in clear idiomatic English.*"
—MANCHESTER GUARDIAN.

"*The notes will be found most useful, both in explain-
ing the structure of the book and in elucidating its
meaning; and, in short, the volume cannot fail to
prove most serviceable to such as may desire to study
minutely, in the light of the latest scientific criticism,
this ancient law-book.*"—SCOTSMAN.

"*The translation and notes are scholarly and sug-
gestive. The translation is specially interesting and
valuable.*"—GLASGOW HERALD.

"*Dr. Driver's name will serve in Britain as a
guarantee of the thoroughness of the scholarship and
fineness of judgment displayed in this volume. . . .
The fruits of immense labour are most reverently and
instructively presented in this fine volume.*"
—ARBROATH HERALD.

"*That the work will be a valuable, indeed an invalu-
able, contribution to the progress of Biblical study,
no one can doubt.*"—GOOD WORDS.

"Any one reading it can see at once how, according to this 'Higher Criticism,' the book has been constructed. . . . The high reputation of the chief editor of this volume for Hebrew scholarship is well known, and naturally claims the most careful study for any work that is issued by him."
    —NORTH BRITISH DAILY MAIL.

"A work which cannot be ignored."
    —CAMBRIDGE INDEPENDENT PRESS.

J. A. Paterson.

THE BOOK OF NUMBERS. Translated, with Notes, by J. A. Paterson, D.D., Professor at the Theological Seminary, Edinburgh.   [*May, 1899.*

G. A. Smith.

THE BOOK OF DEUTERONOMY. Translated, with Notes, by George Adam Smith, D.D., LL.D., Professor of Hebrew and Old Testament Exegesis at the Free Church College, Glasgow.   [*May, 1899.*

W. H. Bennett.

THE BOOK OF JOSHUA. Translated, with Notes, by W. H. Bennett, M.A., Professor of Hebrew and Old Testament Exegesis at Hackney and New Colleges, London.   [*December.*

G. F. Moore.

THE BOOK OF JUDGES. Translated, with Notes, by G. F. Moore, D.D., Professor of Hebrew in Andover Theological Seminary. 98 pp., printed in seven colours (42 pp. translation, 56 pp. notes). Seven full-page illustrations (including a map in colours), twenty illustrations in the Notes. Cloth, gilt top, price 6s. net.   [*Ready.*

"I admire the skill with which the most necessary information on the origin of the book is here com-

municated to the English reader, and the fulness and yet conciseness of the notes. As to the colours which indicate the sources of the existing composite work, I can by no means sympathise with the laughers who have begun to show themselves. If the public are to be enabled to see what analytic criticism comes to, such a plan as Dr. Haupt has devised, and Professor Moore and others have endeavoured to carry out, was indispensable. As a specimen of fine prose I would gladly quote the story of Jephthah's daughter, but it may be enough to invite the reader to get the book, and turn to the passage at once."
—DR. CHEYNE IN "THE EXPOSITOR."

"The translation is in clear, strong, dignified modern English. The explanatory notes are concise, to the point and adequate. The map and illustrations are just what is required to throw light on the book."
—MANCHESTER GUARDIAN.

"Professor G. F. Moore, of Andover, stands in the front rank of Old Testament students. His English rendering is readable, though it looks to faithfulness first and to style only in the second place. His notes are pointed and helpful; his criticism is free and thoroughgoing, without becoming either precipitate or showy."
—CRITICAL REVIEW.

J. Wellhausen, H. Howard Furness.

THE BOOK OF PSALMS. Translated by **J. Wellhausen, D.D.,** Professor of Semitic Languages at Göttingen, and **H. Howard Furness, Ph.D., LL.D.,** Editor of "The Variorum Shakespeare." 224 pp. (161 pp. translation, 63 pp. notes, including an Appendix on the Music of the Ancient Hebrews). Eight full-page illustrations (one in colours), and fifty-three illustrations in the Notes and Appendix. Cloth, gilt top, price 10s. 6d. net.   [*Ready.*

"The most beautiful version of the Hebrew Psalms which exists in our language."
—DR. CHEYNE IN "THE EXPOSITOR."

"The 'Psalms' are translated and edited by Professor Wellhausen. The German translations are rendered into English by Mr. Furness. And the effect is, we can only say, magnificent. Here for the first time the

English reader is enabled to understand obscure places in the Psalms, and at the same time to catch the roll of the rhythm and to feel that the Psalms are poems."—DAILY CHRONICLE.

"The Psalms, which have been translated by the greatest Biblical critic in Europe or the world, Professor Wellhausen, are distinguished externally from the other books by being absolutely colourless. This, of course, does not mean that they are not of very different epochs of Jewish history, and Professor Wellhausen's treatment of these and analogous questions is worthy of the scholar who has done more to throw light upon the composition of the books of the Old Testament than all of his predecessors."
—DAILY TELEGRAPH.

T. K. Cheyne.

THE BOOK OF THE PROPHET ISAIAH.
Translated, with Notes, by **T. K. Cheyne, D.D.**, Oriel Professor of the Interpretation of Holy Scripture at Oxford, and Canon of Rochester. 216 pp., printed in seven colours (128 pp. translation, 88 pp. notes). Nine full-page illustrations and twenty-eight illustrations in Notes. Cloth, gilt top, price 10s. 6d. net.
[*Ready.*

"If the reader of the Polychrome Isaiah feels that he has before him a totally different book from the familiar Isaiah of the English Bible, he will not feel that he has lost, but gained; for while his new Isaiah is far easier to understand, it possesses no less of the inspired passion and power and truth which have always made the Book of Isaiah the favourite book of the Old Testament."—DAILY CHRONICLE.

"By far the most important of the three first volumes which have just seen the light is the Book of Isaiah, by Professor Cheyne, whose previous writings on the Old Testament are widely known and highly appreciated. He is at once the most lucid, dispassionate, and cautious of English scholars, and the uninitiated reader, to whatever school of theology he may belong, can fully commit himself to his guidance."
—DAILY TELEGRAPH.

C. H. Toy.	**THE BOOK OF THE PROPHET EZEKIEL.** Translated, with Notes, by **C. H. Toy, D.D.**, Professor of Hebrew and Lecturer on Biblical Literature in Harvard University. *[December.*

E. T. Bartlett, J. P. Peters, F. W. Farrar.	**THE BIBLE; FOR HOME AND SCHOOL.** Arranged by **Ed. T. Bartlett, M.A.**, Dean of the Protestant Episcopal Divinity School in Philadelphia, and **John P. Peters, Ph.D.**, Professor of the Old Testament Languages and Literature in the Protestant Episcopal Divinity School in Philadelphia. With Introduction by **Rev. F. W. Farrar, D.D.**, Dean of Canterbury. In ten monthly parts, 1s. each. In One Vol., cloth, 8vo, 10s. 6d. DEAN FARRAR says:—"*An important contribution to the training of the young in truths which God has revealed to us by His Holy Book, as it is read in the light of that advancing knowledge which is itself a part of the Divine enlightenment which He vouchsafes to all mankind, as always, fragmentarily and multifariously, yet progressively 'in many parts and in many manners.'*"

W. H. Bennett, W. F. Adeney.	**THE BIBLE STORY.** Re-told for Young People. The OLD TESTAMENT STORY, by **W. H. Bennett, M.A.** (sometime Fellow of St. John's College, Cambridge), Professor of Hebrew and Old Testament Exegesis at Hackney and New Colleges, London. The NEW TESTAMENT STORY by **W. F. Adeney, M.A.**, Professor of New Testa-

W. H. Bennett, W. F. Adeney.

ment Greek Exegesis, at New College, London. With illustrations and 4 maps.

This book is designed to supply the want of such a presentation of the narratives contained in the Bible as shall be suitable for the reading of young people. The results of recent Historical Research and Biblical Criticism are brought to bear on the story, to throw light on it and also to prevent misapprehensions. The book is reduced to reasonable dimensions, by the omission of those portions of the narrative which are less suitable for young people, and also of incidents not essential to the story. In this way the salient features are emphasized and some sense of proportion observed, while there is scope for those dramatic elements which have always fascinated young readers of the Bible.

———

Fourth Edition (completing 12,000 copies).

W. F. Adeney.

HOW TO READ THE BIBLE. Hints for Sunday-School Teachers and other Bible Students.

By **Walter F. Adeney**, M.A., Professor of New Testament Exegesis, &c., New College, London, and Author of "The Theology of the New Testament" (Theological Educator), "The Canticles and Lamentations," "Ezra, Nehemiah, and Esther" (Expositor's Bible), &c. Pott 8vo, in paper, 1s.; in cloth, 1s. 6d.

"This little book aims at being a most elementary introduction to the study of the Bible. To many readers much of it will appear to be a perfectly superfluous reiteration of the most obvious truths. But it

is a singular fact that warnings that never need to be uttered, and directions that never need to be laid down, in regard to the study of any other work in the world's literature, are imperatively called for to prevent the student of Scripture from being ensnared by the most outrageous devices of misinterpretation."

R. F. Horton.

Dr. Horton on Romanism.

ENGLAND'S DANGER.

By **Robert F. Horton, M.A., D.D.** Fourth Edition. Fcap. 8vo, 6d.

Minnie Elligott.

A HELPING HAND TO MOTHERS.

By **Minnie Elligott.** Fcap. 8vo, paper, 6d.

The AUTHOR says: *"In submitting this little book to Mothers I hope I am rendering a slight service to those who, while earnestly desirous of bringing up their children on healthy principles, are frequently at a loss how to act, simply from lack of experience. The first baby is often the victim of divers experiments which would never be tried were its wants and requirements properly understood. I have endeavoured to show what these are, and to point out how the children of parents whose means are limited may be as well trained and cared for as those of mothers and fathers in affluent circumstances."*

R. A. Armstrong.

FAITH AND DOUBT IN THE CENTURY'S POETS.

By **Richard A. Armstrong, B.A.** Fcap. 8vo, 2s. 6d.

Prose and Verse by Mary E. Manners, H. E. Inman, Kate Lee, A. Dixon, S. D. Constance, and many others.

Illustrated by Louis Wain, E. A. Mason, Felix Leigh, Harry Dixon, A. T. Elwes, T. Cromwell Lawrence, G. Stoddart, &c.

THE ROSEBUD ANNUAL, 1899. With about 200 Original Illustrations. In handsome cloth binding, 4s.

As a Reward Book, Birthday or Christmas Present for a child, "The Rosebud Annual" still stands unrivalled. The short stories in prose and verse are full of healthy humour, and while free from goody-goodiness, convey many a lesson in a quiet way. Every picture in the book was specially drawn for it, and nearly all the birds of the air, the beasts of the field and the fish in the sea are represented in various comical attitudes. There are also songs with music.

What the Papers say about THE ROSEBUD:

THE TIMES: "*Few more lively.*"

DAILY GRAPHIC: "*Vast resources in the way of amusement.*"

DAILY NEWS: "*Looks particularly attractive.*"

WESTMINSTER GAZETTE: "*One of the best.*"

DAILY TELEGRAPH: "*Splendidly printed.*"

STAR: "*Storehouse of innocent humour and gaiety.*"

PALL MALL GAZETTE: "*No more charming picture-book.*"

SCOTSMAN: "*That pleasant and well-known nursery monthly.*"

LIVERPOOL POST: "*A treasure of delight.*"

LEEDS MERCURY: "*Fascinating.*"

BRADFORD OBSERVER: "*Full of fun and laughter.*"

ABERDEEN FREE PRESS: "*Ideal.*"

BRISTOL MERCURY: *Delightful. . . admirable little magazine.*"

GLASGOW HERALD: "*Sure of a rapturous welcome.*"

DUNDEE ADVERTISER: "*Crammed full of good things.*"

BIRMINGHAM POST: "*Well adapted for very little folks.*"

NEWCASTLE CHRONICLE: "*None more entertaining.*"

NEWCASTLE LEADER: "*Well worth the money.*"

DERBY GAZETTE: "*Charmingly got up.*"

HUDDERSFIELD EXAMINER: "*We know of nothing better.*"

OXFORD CHRONICLE: "*Bound to be treasured.*"

MIDLAND FREE PRESS: "*An old and ever-welcome friend.*"

PRESTON GUARDIAN: "*The Nursery 'Punch.'*"

LLOYD'S NEWS: "*A veritable mine of wealth for the juveniles.*"

PUNCH: "*Gorgeously gay.*"

ST. JAMES'S BUDGET: "*Sure to be a favourite.*"

BOOK AND NEWS TRADE GAZETTE: "*Will always find a big sale.*"

Lightning Source UK Ltd.
Milton Keynes UK
UKHW02f1244150718
325723UK00005B/115/P

9 781298 041401